Loving Wings

*Stewardesses and Pilots who
Conquered the Skies of
Yesteryear for Today's
Fantastic Aviation Industry*

By
Marty Ruffin Gardner

Eloquent Books
New York, New York

Eloquent Books
An imprint of AEG Publishing Group
845 Third Avenue, 6th Floor – 6016
New York, NY 10022
www.eloquentbooks.com

ISBN: 978-1-60693-915-4   1-60693-915-7

Printed in the United States of America

Book Design: D. Johnson, Dedicated Business Solutions, Inc.

Abstract

Loving Wings is a lively account of stewardesses encountering passengers and problems since 1940 when pilots declared, "Adding a woman to the crew is about as sensible as removing one of the wings."

Praying and pushing are just some of the methods flight attendants have used over the decades as they have gone from:

- ✦ Serving a box lunch with a shiny red apple,
- ✦ To accommodating six brave air travelers,
- ✦ To corralling a pet snake slithering beneath the seats of 385 petrified passengers 37,000 feet in the air,
- ✦ To stifling blood chilling screams of a lady passenger when the stewardess took away her marijuana,
- ✦ To conspiring in plans to overthrow the cockpit.

Loving Wings encompasses the Forties through the Seventies, from the beginning of stewardesses, to the beginning of stewardesses becoming pilots aboard your flight.

Dedicated to:

My amazing loved ones: A family extra-ordinaire.
With grateful editorial acknowledgment to
Bobbi Ray Madry.

Table of Contents

Foreword

In 1940, a progressive airline decided to add someone to be inside the cabin to take care of passengers. Air travelers were beginning to be bold enough to travel through the skies. No longer were airplanes used just to carry mail across the countryside, using tops of barns and dirt roads as navigational aids to cross state lines in a faster way. Air travelers came aboard, and with these brave souls, also came air hostesses or stewardesses.

The first stewardesses had to be brave, adventuresome, personable and capable. But they met a lot of opposition from the barnstorming pilots that controlled the air.

Loving Wings presents the first decades of stewardesses in a lively account of their trials and tribulations, their personal lives, and their adventures on the ground and in the air.

The Forties

Choose an exciting career—a career in the sky.

If you qualify, join America's most exciting new profession for young women. A whole new adventure awaits the forward looking girl of today.

Be an airline stewardess.

Start at a salary of $90.00 a month. While you are with our Southaire Corporation your salary can go upwards in excess of $110.00 a month.

Basic requirements include:

You must be a registered nurse . . . must be single and never have been married . . . have unimpaired vision (glasses are not permissible) . . . must have a clear complexion . . . must be attractive . . . must have even, white teeth . . . must present a neat appearance . . . must have a pleasing personality . . . must be of high moral character . . . must be in good physical condition (an entrance examination and regular 6 month examinations are required) . . . and must be willing to travel.

You must be 22 to 25 years of age, 5 feet to 5 feet 5 inches in height, with weight in proportion to height, with maximum weight 120 pounds (airline average is 110 pounds).

If you meet our qualifications, we will arrange a personal interview with you.

On March 15, 1940, Southaire Corporation spread its wings with a new airplane, the 14 passenger DC-2, and something unique and very attractive—its first stewardess. Graduation ceremonies for nine trainees were headlined in bold type. The girls' smiles brightened all Southern newspapers.

Public relations people were jubilant over the reception to this novel service aboard an aircraft. However, management was skeptical, and pilots were stunned and furious. They argued that adding a woman to the crew was about as sensible as removing one of the wings.

Chapter 1—Girls, that is
an Air-O-Plane!

Pauline O'Shannon was the most beautiful of the nine trainees. Her perky turned-up nose, auburn curls and aquamarine eyes caused men to think, *Wow, I'd like to get to know her better*. However, after getting to know Pauline, the impression changed to, *Ouch! That girl is ornery as a hornet*.

McLain (Mac) Saranata was in the audience of the original stewardess graduation exercises. Every pilot with Southaire not flying that day was in attendance. Those nine girls were scrutinized from every angle. Mac's position was strategic. He wanted to examine the specimens before him while his cohorts imitated his contemptuous expression. For a brief instant, Pauline caught his gaze. Then, with a flick of velvet eyelashes, she dismissed him from her tumultuous thoughts.

In that second, the challenge had been hurled. Mac caught it squarely. He immediately knew he would have to convince that uppity chick she was only a woman. Whatever else, the mainstay rule of Southaire's cockpits was that the Captain is boss!

In 1940, pilots were crop-dusting, barnstorming show aerialists. They were hard-hitting, weathered guys in a daredevil profession. They earned their right to pilot commercial aircraft by suffering apprenticeship at the hands of fate and luck. By the time they received their wings, most had already participated in feats used in textbooks as illustrations on how to be a good pilot.

Mac, at age 25, was the leader of the best.

After the pinning of their wings by Mr. A. F. Williams, the founder and president of Southaire Corporation, nine young women were officially welcomed into the growing family.

Miss Jean Canons, chief stewardess and instructor for the girls, held out a stewardess hat containing nine slips of folded paper. Seniority was determined by a drawing. The most senior, number one would have the best flight rotation or group of flights. At that moment, the excited girls didn't really care. They were anxious to be on any flight. Some had never been on an airplane.

Pauline had never flown until she had been chosen as one of the candidates for the coveted position of stewardess. She had spent the last quarter of her 22 years gaining knowledge and experience in her chosen profession, nursing. She was working as a surgical nurse when her supervisor selected her to be interviewed by Jean Canons for possible employment in a new capacity, a flight stewardess for Southaire Corporation. Miss Canons was traveling throughout the country carefully selecting nurses recommended by hospital supervisors.

Despite being a surgical nurse and working with unconscious patients, Pauline showed in the interview that she was adept at handling alert people as well. Facing twenty judgmental executives seated around a walnut conference table who were watching her for any weaknesses, she remained controlled and charming. They interrogated her for more than five hours on every aspect of her education, experience, ambitions and her handling of hypothetical situations.

Even after her first airplane trip to Atlanta for the interview, Pauline still couldn't believe the promise of such a new career unlike any she had ever heard of. She shook her head in astonishment. *These people from this airline are actually going to pay me $90 a month to fly on airplanes and look after passengers. I only earn $60 as a nurse. Move over birds, here I come.*

Adventurously, at the end of graduation exercises, Pauline placed a manicured hand into the stewardess cap and plucked seniority #7. With it went the Atlanta, Georgia to Fort Worth, Texas run for six months. Her thoughts about the future were jumbled. *Hope I don't get sick. Hope I have a nice crew. Hope we can get along for six months. Mr. Williams told us we have to make the pilots like us. But they resent us so.*

A flash of O'Shannon temper surfaced. *The heck with them. They had better worry about whether I like them. Oth-*

*erwise, I might learn to fly, take over their job and really
give them something to resent. Hope I don't get sick. I've
heard there are real cowboys and cattle roaming the streets
of Fort Worth, Texas. Oh, how exciting! I can't wait to see
it. I wonder how my passengers will like me. I'll love them,
every one of them. I love them already. I love everybody. I
can't believe this is happening to me. I don't dare get sick.
I'm a nurse. Nurses don't get sick. No, I'm not a nurse. I'm
an airline stewardess!*

A commanding, raspy voice intruded on Pauline's
thoughts. "Which one's the Fort Worth gal? Which one of
you queens is gonna fly on my air-o-plane? C'mon, c'mon.
One of youse babes drew number 7. That's me! That's my
run."

McLain Saranata kept his eyes on Pauline. His gaze was
betraying his self-imposed superiority. *Man, she is gorgeous*,
he thought. "Hey you, hey skirt, what number ya got?"

With startled directness, she focused on his strong, weathered, heavy-browed eyes. "Did you address me, sir?"

"Yeah. What's yer rotation?"

"My rotation?"

"Yer rotation! Yer run! Yer flights! Didn't they learn you
anything in that so-called hostess school?"

"Of course, sir. It was a most worthwhile, educational experience." Behind her aqua-eyed gaze and upper-class dia-
logue, Pauline was thinking, *Jean Canons warned us about
oddball people we would encounter. I think I've just met my
first!* "Are you with the airline, sir?"

"Sir! Scmhire! My name is McLain Saranata. Captain Saranata! Captain on the Fort Worth rotation. What's yours?"

"My rotation or my name, sir?"

"Cripes! Whatever ya wanna be called . . . in public, that
is! Do you think you can remember? After all, it's been a
whole five minutes since you drew a rotation and it's been
like ten minutes since A. F. pinned on your wings and announced your name."

"Pauline Elizabeth O'Shannon, sir, Chicago University,
Masters in Nursing, Oakland Training Center, Head Surgical

Nurse at Mercy Hospital and number seven seniority in the historic first stewardess class of Southaire Corporation."

"Pheweeee! I'll bet cha chew Dentyne for bad breath, too."

"Stewardesses are not permitted to chew gum, smoke or remove their hats in public, sir."

"Well, baby doll", Mac glared, "You better obey those rules because I'm your commander-in-chief for the next six months. One slip-up on my air-o-plane and you're the ex of all them things you just said you was."

Festivities closed in around them. Merriment was contagious. Handshakes and hugs engulfed the nine young women representing each of the Southern states served by the Southaire Corporation. Public relations people beamed with pride. Management eyed management with palatable questions in mid air. *Would this new service succeed?* Pilots mentally examined female derrieres and fantasized about the ones which would fit nicely upon their laps. The young women sparkled with celebrity fever and promised to remain friends forever and ever.

Significant progress was launched in a new industry. Pioneers in this beginning of air travel were outwardly adventuresome, while inwardly they were trying to quell their anxiety.

Chapter 2—Outhouses and
VFR Instrumentation

One ramshackle room housed Southaire's operations, pilots lounge and flight control services. Walls were unfinished concrete decorated with phone numbers, wind velocities of past journeys and numerical columns totaling poker winnings on account. A time weathered counter separated the technical division from the fly boys.

In the lounge area, five cockpit seats displaced from their original setting were haphazardly grouped around an upturned baggage bin. Two weeks flying pay was lost or won at this recreation site, while interested postal clerks, baggage agents, and pilot-worshiping overgrown farm boys made up the gum-popping, smoking cheering section.

Georgia rain pelted the tin roof and followed grooves on oily window panes to create a small lake at each entrance to the building. Muddy tracks carpeted the pilot's side of the room.

In the more proficient, technical section on the other side of the counter, maps, charts and updated instruments more than filled the space. Range stations for VFR aircraft control were prominent on land maps and weather charts. Railroad tracks were carefully illustrated. Some smart guy (no one would say for sure it was Mac) had grabbed an unattended period of time behind the counter to display an artistic talent. Cows, horses and outhouses were dotted throughout the Southaire route system.

At 4:30 a.m. in black, misty March weather, Pauline O'Shannon approached the building. Fastidiously, she tried to step over the puddle by the door. Her arrival was anticipated and over half the night personnel of the whole terminal was crowded into the room. Bets were placed on her being a no-show. The weather was lousy.

Looking around outside, Pauline found a board, placed it over the puddle and made her entrance on schedule. The plank was to remain over the spot for months and was used gratefully by all airline feet.

Within minutes the crowd dispersed to positions necessary to accommodate early travelers. On this morning, six brave souls were venturing aboard Southaire's # AM-23, so named for the mail route over which the flight traveled.

Tommy Jensen, copilot, had been unable to attend stewardess graduation ceremonies the previous day. However, had he been there, he would have remained in the background. Tommy was shy, a cursed personality trait he was forever trying to overcome. Upon meeting Pauline, his fair complexion broke out in nervous hives.

Pauline took one look and thought, *Lord! It looks like this guy's got the measles.*

Operations agent Thornton announced, "The weather tower says it's clearing west. AM-23 will depart on time or thereabouts. Miss O'Shannon, Captain Saranata wants you to get started on your duties. He is up in the weather tower and will be down shortly. Tommy, he wants you to start filing the flight plan, then load cargo."

Tommy offered timidly, "Would you like me to walk you to the ship, miss?"

Pauline, fearful of contagious measles, hastily smiled and moved quickly. "Oh no! No thank you." Gathering her suitcase, purse and clipboard, she waved to her audience and went out the door.

Once on board, exhilaration warmed her chilled body. She stood just inside the entrance and looked uphill at the fourteen passenger seats, then beyond into the cockpit with its mysterious gadgets. She smelled the newness of the plane and grinned.

Speaking aloud to the empty interior, her voice resonated with excitement. "Good morning! I am Pauline O'Shannon, your flight stewardess aboard Southaire Corporation's number AM-23. I am a registered nurse and capable of administering to all your needs." She shook her head. *That doesn't come first. What did Jean Canons teach us? I know I have a*

*thousand different articles to check before each flight. I can't
think of one thing to check. I just want to shout good morning to the world and praise the lord for getting me this far.*

Agent Thornton poked his head in the door. "Ready for
the box lunches and vacuum bottles?"

"Yes sir. Ready."

"Is your medical kit okay? Got your barbiturates and
sleeping pills?" He stepped inside.

"I haven't checked yet, sir."

"Do you have plenty of comfort bags and your official airline guide?" He was itemizing as he counted on his fingers.

"I really don't know, sir."

"Would you like me to help you this morning, Miss
O'Shannon?"

"I would be eternally grateful, sir. However, Captain Saranata made it perfectly clear I am to attend to my own duties,
sir."

"Then why don't you get your training notes out and
briefly review them before Captain Saranata boards, You
have enough time. Personally, I think you girls are the best
thing to happen to this airline." With a conspiratorial wink,
he withdrew his head from the doorway.

By the time the six travelers approached the two steps of
the new Douglas Corporation 2 aircraft, Pauline was standing at attention in the light rain, holding an umbrella for
them. They all knew who she was. There had been no other
talk inside the terminal except about her. To her delight, the
men removed their hats and greeted her with a "Good morning, Miss O'Shannon".

Once the six men were seated, Captain Saranata filled the
interior with his bulk. Tommy strode like a shadow behind
him. Both pilots uttered a brisk "Good morning" in general
to everyone and went directly to the cockpit where they proceeded to fascinate the passengers by flipping switches and
turning knobs.

Agent Thornton called from the entrance door, "Miss
O'Shannon, here is the flight plan and weather report. After

you read the weather forecast to your passengers, give both papers to Captain Saranata."

A young, fast-moving man with a red press card stuck in the rim of his hat band rudely brushed Thornton aside and hopped into the cabin. "Miss, hey miss, I'm from the Atlanta Times. I need a photograph and statement for our edition. I overslept and if I don't turn in this story, I'll lose my job. Please let me take a picture and ask some questions. I won't be long. Please?"

The passengers turned in their seats at this unexpected development. The newspaper man dropped to one knee and appealed to the six men. "Please?"

One passenger called, "Go ahead, Miss O'Shannon. He shouldn't lose his job." The other passengers nodded.

Having their blessings, Pauline smiled and posed. Agent Thornton stood in bewilderment. Captain Saranata turned from his left-hand cockpit seat to see what was causing the delay on his flight. His face reflected angry disbelief.

Pauline began answering the young man's questions. "Of course I'm happy to be an airline stewardess. Yes, I'm a tiny bit apprehensive. This is my second trip aboard flying aircraft. Yes, the lunch boxes today are tied with pink ribbon in honor of the occasion."

"What in blue blazes is going on in my air-o-plane?" Mac's question came through gritted teeth, as he stood behind her.

Thornton retreated. The reporter folded his notebook, tipped his hat, blew Pauline a kiss and left. Pauline, unruffled, turned and answered, "Publicity, sir. Publicity to sell more tickets aboard your flights, sir."

"Do you mind if my air-o-plane takes to the air where it belongs?"

"I believe that will be of utmost importance to this venture, sir."

Mac brushed past her, grabbed the handle of the entrance door to the DC-2 aircraft, slammed it shut, locked it, snatched the papers from her hand and commanded, "Sit down and fasten your seat belt."

Airborne, the craft bounced in turbulent skies. Pauline held onto seats as she climbed up and down the aisle of the tilted DC-2.

A seasoned traveler informed her, "The towns I like best are ones which have their names painted on the tops of big buildings." He pointed out the window. Pauline leaned over to look. In bright lettering below was Birmingham. Pauline was thrilled. "I believe I like those towns best, too."

Pauline noticed another nervous passenger, although he had earlier assured her that he was not a first-time traveler. Having caught her attention, he asked "What did they teach you in hostess school, Miss O'Shannon?"

"We had six weeks of training in meteorology, the routes traveled, craft equipment, emergency procedures . . ." He flinched at the word emergency, but she quickly continued. "Grooming, range station signals, and before we graduated, we had to draw, free hand, a map of the United States and show all commercial airline plane stops. If you need help in planning a continuing trip, I can route you to your final destination using my knowledge about other airline services."

Suddenly, behind her was the dreaded sound of an airsick person. As she moved quickly to assist him with a cold wet towel, she told herself, *hang on. Don't dare get sick. Be detached. It's only a patient. It's only a sick patient. Be a nurse. Attend to a patient. Don't be a queasy female who's going to get nauseated if he doesn't stop.'*

In a few minutes the embarrassed man closed his eyes and leaned against a pillow. Pauline had convinced him air sickness wasn't fatal. She checked seat belts. They were coming in for their first stop in the leapfrog journey to Fort Worth.

When the door opened, Pauline was handed a bouquet of red roses. A rotund man with a watch chain hanging across his vest stepped forward and introduced himself as the Mayor. A speech was made by His Honor heralding stewardess service aboard the progressive and fine Southaire Corporation. An emphatic ending to his speech declared, "A. F. Williams is a progressive and forward-thinking leader in this industry." A photographer came forward and took several pictures of the Mayor and Pauline at the door of the airplane.

Amidst applause, Mac tried vainly to push his way out the door which was intentionally blocked by a radiant Pauline who was in no hurry to end the accolades.

Chapter 3—Controllable Pitch Propellers, Uncontrollable Pilots

The curious crowd cheered Pauline, Mac, the two deplaning passengers, and even the one bewildered new rider as he stepped on board. Flustered, Mac sternly reprimanded the small crew about the necessities of maintaining schedules and of the importance of AM-23 departing on time. Hearing Mac bellow commands reminded Pauline of a tyrannical, disliked doctor she had once worked for.

As the flight leveled off, Mac thought about simpler flying days. He was flattered by the publicity his flight was receiving, but it was exasperating that one female could cause so much commotion. *I know she's smart. But a young, pretty gal like that ought to be home with a husband and children instead of playing Florence Nightingale on my air-o-plane. I tried to tell A. F. girls ain't gonna be nothing but trouble.* He turned from the cockpit to watch her work in the cabin. *I don't know what all she is supposed to do. I guess she's doing okay. At least she's staying busy.*

On those first trips, the only people who really knew the duties of an airline stewardess were Jean Canons, chief stewardess, the nine trainees she had just graduated, and an occasional agent like Thornton in Atlanta. The passengers didn't know. The pilots were completely befuddled. The girls knew . . . and what they knew was that it wasn't to be a cutie-pie, glamorous job. They had to use their brain and they have to have tremendous physical stamina.

The onboard passenger was a 'first rider'. Tucked into his seat, buckled in, pillow at his neck, blanket about his knees to ward off the March chill, he started asking questions that showed he was fearful. "What kind of a motor does this thing have?"

Squatting beside his seat, Pauline smiled. "Mr. Ladspole, this DC-2 has 1250-horsepower twin engines with controllable pitch propellers and will cruse at 165 miles per hour."

He gulped. "Do you know how to fly, Miss O'Shannon?"

"No sir. But I do know quite a bit about this aircraft, sir. We studied operation of aircraft in stewardess training. We even learned how to gas equipment, Mr. Ladspole."

Impressed with Pauline's competency, he began to relax. "You mean you know how to put gasoline in this airplane?"

"Yes sir. We spent considerable time in the hanger while this craft was being inspected for Southaire service. As the mechanics peered into stabilizer and aileron equipment, so did we. When nacelle and cowling were removed to verify inner workings, we were alongside studying and memorizing the parts. Our training has been most extensive. Be assured the Southaire Corporation has prepared its stewardess service quite thoroughly. Would you like a sweet roll and beverage? A thermal bottle of hot coffee was placed on board just before we departed."

"I don't want to eat it, but could I have a roll as a souvenir of my first flight?"

"Certainly, Mr. Ladspole. I'll wrap one in a napkin for you. If you will excuse me, sir, I'll see if any of my other passengers need help."

"Please come back and talk to me some more." He was beginning to tense up again.

"I will, Mr. Ladspole. Since you are going all the way to Fort Worth, we will be together all day today."

A few minutes later, Pauline stuck her head inside the cockpit and called above the roar, "Would you like coffee and a roll?"

Tommy unbuckled his seat belt, bent slightly and moved to her. She noticed his measles were no longer prominent. "Miss O'Shannon, I'll get them. Before today, serving everyone on board was part of my duties." He moved around her and headed for the back of the plane.

While the copilot was in the buffet area, the five passengers turned quizzically back and forth to watch her in the cockpit and him in the cabin. Leaning toward a passenger across the aisle, Mr. Ladspole reassured him. "She knows as much 'bout this airplane as he does."

Standing by the cockpit doorway, Pauline heard McLain yell. "Do you want to see it?"

She stepped inside. "See what, sir?"

"Do you want to see my cockpit?" Mac was secure in his space. Here, he was all about positive action, and he showed it with every gesture and every word. "Step forward. Look at these instruments. This is the altimeter. We're at 8,000 feet. Here, here. Put on the earphone."

He handed her a set from Tommy's instrument panel. She held them a minute. "Listen to the range station signal comin' in from Jackson, Mississippi. Ya wanna hear that dot da dot? You listen. That's how we fly blind. Those signals are set up every 90 miles. There's also a beacon light turnin' on top of every one of those range stations. Now if we was going north, the signal would be da dot da. Right in the center of these signals you will hear a bbbbbeeeee. That means we are on perfect course. We can fly in clouds and at night by listening to the signals and watching fer the beacon lights. What do you think of that?"

Pauline was amazed, not by what he was telling her because she already knew all about range stations, but by the animated expression on his weather-beaten features as he presented his discourse on blind flying. This was the most human he had seemed to her so far. *Perhaps*, she thought, *perhaps we might be friends before these six months are over on this rotation.*

"Those are our checkpoints. When we fly over, we report by radio our altitude, ya know, how high we is flying, how fast and what the weather is doing. All us pilots do that. Then the range stations give us back reports from other pilots. It's a pretty good set-up. Keeps us informed. How about that?" He motioned to the earphones, then leaned over and helped Pauline adjust the earphones over her stewardess cap.

She listened a minute, heard a constant bbbbbeeeee, knew they were precision performing, then removed the ear phones and handed them back to Mac. He replaced them on the copilot's side of the panel.

Watching his smug facial expression, Pauline knew she wouldn't be the one to tell him they had learned all about range stations in stewardess training and that it was required knowledge before they could graduate.

"Thank you, Captain Saranata. Would you like me to bring you some coffee and a roll?"

"Naw. Tommy will bring me something. Before you, that was his job. Guess the next thing will be women copilots."

Retreating, she called out, "Oh no sir! Never on your flights."

In Jackson, Mississippi, a welcoming committee met AM-23. A bouquet of camellias was presented to Pauline. Photographs were taken and Pauline was asked to say a few words for the radio audience about a new career in the sky.

It was late evening before they checked into the Worth Hotel in downtown Fort Worth, Texas. The trip from Atlanta, Georgia had taken ten hours with eight stops. Pauline had seen no cattle or wagons on the streets but there had been horses and cowboys. Pauline was ushered into a room at the hotel, two floors removed from the gentlemen pilots. A gala banquet was planned for later in honor of the occasion with Southaire Corporation officials as hosts.

In her Western decorated room, Pauline stretched out on her bed with arms flung above her head and kicked chunky shoes across the room. A low moan escaped from her mouth as she reveled in the solitude. *I have never been so exhausted in my lifetime. I don't believe I have the stamina required for this job. Even my hair is tired. I have walked all the way from Georgia to Texas. But I must get up. I have to appear downstairs at a reception in 45 minutes. Well, Mr. and Mrs. America, and all the ships at sea, will she do it? Will Miss Pauline Elizabeth O'Shannon emerge forthwith or will she slide down into her bath water never to be seen again? That is the subject of tonight's news. Stand by, America.* She rolled over on the bed and started peeling off her heavy wool uniform as she headed for the bathroom.

Festivities lasted well into the evening. Officials of Fort Worth pronounced stewardess service a resounding success. City fathers told news people, "Meacham Field is honored to have Southaire Corporation serve as a passenger carrier for this area. Proposed terminal plans are a wonderful incentive for Southaire to increase flight and stewardess service tenfold to this city where the West begins."

When she fell in bed at midnight, Pauline didn't care if cowboys, cattle or even bears roamed the streets. All that mattered to her this first night of her first trip was that she didn't have to roam one more step.

Chapter 4—Muddy Monroe
and Mrs. Weeks

Within a month, a second stewardess class search was implemented. Publicity was powerful and 1,100 applications were submitted.

President A. F. Williams was a welcomed passenger on AM-23 one spring day. Pauline brightly discussed current events with him as if they were old friends. With no precedent to follow, both agreed that stewardess service was definitely necessary in the continued growth of Southaire.

When Pauline gave Mr. Williams his white box lunch tied with a string and containing cold fried chicken, potato salad, bread and butter sandwich and a shiny red apple, he gave her the apple to save for herself as a snack.

Personnel were on a first-name basis in the Southaire family. If there was a personal problem, most likely it was discussed with A. F. Williams. His door was always open and his wrinkled grin welcomed many a timid entrant into his unpretentious office. Photographs of A. F. and his employees lined the walls. Periodicals of pilot flying feats were framed and there was a good in-the-air photo of McLain Saranata at the controls of a ten passenger Lockheed Electra made in 1936. The closeness and genuine caring was evident and touched all Southaire employees.

On AM-23, the diverse crew merged into a team. Stewardess service became routine. Mac shared boardinghouse gossip with fellow pilots claiming that such and such stewardess was better looking than the rest. On flights, professional duties were precisely performed. Any deviation from the norm was quickly adjusted by the skillful job training of Mac, Pauline or Tommy Jensen.

During a rainy week in June, the AM-23 team experienced their first emergency. Runways and fields were soaked to capacity and the Mississippi Delta section of the country was virtually flooded. In an attempted landing at Monroe, Louisiana, hydraulic fluid was lost and the DC-2 went off the end of a runway, the wheels hopelessly bogged in the mud.

All three crew members worked to evacuate the seven passengers. A windy thunderstorm hampered Pauline as she tried to get her people out the door. Mac hopped into the mud and offered to carry a woman passenger to the end of the runway where emergency equipment was waiting.

The woman turned to Pauline and said, "Ah don't want him to take me in his arms across that field. Will you' all just help me down? Ah can walk by myself. My husband would think ah was a fool if ah let another man carry me around."

"Certainly, ma'am. I'll tell Captain Saranata to move out of your way." She hollered above the wind, "Captain Saranata, Mrs. Weeks doesn't want you to help her. Just move aside, please."

Touching his cap as a gesture of service, he stepped out of the way. Mrs. Weeks started out the door, tripped and fell. Embarrassed, she quickly recovered and brushed away Mac's offer of help. She took off running across the field. Her husband quickly followed her.

When all passengers were safely inside the terminal, an ambulance driver approached the crew.

"Miss O'Shannon, that Mrs. Weeks is in the back of my ambulance. She believes she has a broken leg."

Mac boomed. "Broken leg! You're kidding! The way that dame took off across that field, I'd swear she was a distance runner for Mississippi State."

"You may have to do just that, sir. Mrs. Weeks is yelling to everyone that Miss O'Shannon pushed her out of the airplane."

Pauline's aqua eyes reflected red shock. "I what? That's preposterous!" She turned to her captain in disbelief.

McLain protectively took her arm. "Miss O'Shannon, uh, Pauline, did you push Mrs. Weeks?"

She jerked in anger. "Of course not! Most assuredly I did not push that woman from the airplane. Even the suggestion that I did is ridiculous!"

The ambulance driver turned to leave. "You better keep saying that miss, because I got a feeling you're gonna get sued, especially if they find something wrong with Mrs. Week's leg. She and her husband are creating a big commotion. I gotta go. I just wanted to let you know what's happening."

Mac was staring at the flustered Pauline and thinking how beautiful she was when she was mad. She was furious. O'Shannon temperament came through in every syllable as she exclaimed, "I absolutely do not believe this!"

Tommy tried to reassure her. With a crimson complexion, he ventured, "I was right beside you, Miss O'Shannon. I know you did not shove Mrs. Weeks. I'll swear to it in court."

Pauline touched his sleeve. "Thank you, Tommy. You surely are a fine person." His gulp could be heard all over the terminal.

Eight hours later when AM-22, the east-bound flight to Atlanta from Fort Worth, came through on its course, McLain, Pauline and Tommy boarded as passengers. The crippled AM-23 would need extensive repairs to its wheel base after the mud dried and the plane could be moved closer to the Monroe airport hanger.

After the flight was airborne, Mac sat moodily staring out a passenger window. A familiar voice interrupted his thoughts. "Captain Saranata, would you like coffee?"

Pauline was standing before him smiling. "I'm helping serve this leg. I couldn't sit as a passenger and let Jenny do all the work. Do you remember Jenny? She was in my class."

"Nope. Never paid much attention to that class 'cept you." His heart was doing a rapid beat.

"Why, sir, I'm taking that as a compliment."

"Sure, sure! Go ahead."

Bewildered, Pauline stared at him. Her steady gaze made him flinch inwardly. He quickly averted his brown betraying eyes to stare at the cumulus cloud formations through the window beyond the wing tip.

"I assume you don't want coffee?"

"Naw." He wouldn't look at her.

After standing before him for a couple more seconds, Pauline slowly made her way to the buffet and got herself a cup of coffee, then went back to her seat. *That was strange. He seems to be softening. He must be feeling sorry for me. That crazy Mrs. Weeks. Why on earth would she think I would push her? She just got confused and the whole thing will soon be forgotten. Captain Saranata was sweet to say that about my class. He's an unusual person. I guess that's his way of cheering me. I'll never forget the first time I met him at graduation. I thought he was a real oddball and I guess I still think so but in a different way now. He's a sweet oddball.*

When the crew deplaned in Atlanta, Agent Thornton informed the trio, "Mr. Williams wants you to come to his office." As a true disciple of Southaire's family structure and closeness, he softened the announcement. "A. F. just wants the facts concerning your mishap this morning."

Leaving Williams' office after the session with Southaire officials, Mac wanted to talk to her. As they were walking down the steps, he stopped her by grabbing her arm, nearly causing Pauline to fall. Abruptly, she demanded "What's the matter with you?"

"Do you want to go grab a bite to eat?"

"You almost cause me to break my neck to ask me that?"

"I just thought of it. Ya wanna?"

"No thank you, sir."

He let go of her arm and followed her down the steps. "Ya wanna ride home?"

"No thank you, sir."

"Well, see ya in three days Miss O'Shannon."

As she walked around the building toward the terminal, Mac felt frustrated. *What's the matter with her? What did I do? Sir! Cripes. You'd think after all this time, she'd at least call me Mac.* Realizing he was thinking aloud, he quickly sprinted toward his 1940 Chevy Roadster with white wall tires and a chrome angel on the hood.

A month later Mrs. Weeks' case was on the Fulton County courthouse docket. She sued for total disability in her right leg as a result of being pushed from an airplane, flight AM-23 of the Southaire Corporation. The case named stewardess Pauline Elizabeth O'Shannon as the person directly responsible with indirect negligence on the part of pilots Saranata and Jensen. Mrs. Weeks was in a wheelchair. All participants testified. Pauline and her pilots were found innocent.

Mac invited Pauline and Tommy to a celebration supper. Tommy Jensen had met another stewardess, a likeable brunette, who did not cause him to have hives because of his shyness. Therefore, after adjournment of the court case, he declined a crew celebration in favor of an evening with his revered lady. Pauline and Mac went alone to the Henry O'Grady where they spent a pleasant evening in the candle glow discovering mutual idiosyncrasies. Discussing their backgrounds, plans for the future, and trivialities, they shared an attack of uncontrollable giggles when Mac self-consciously dropped his napkin ring and they watched it roll right to the feet of a pompous maître-d.

Pauline experienced surprising amorous thoughts of Mac periodically during the summer and inwardly declared to herself it was admiration for him as a good captain. 'Sweet oddball' in her thoughts was replaced by 'sweet guy'. He took her to see *Gone with the Wind* at the Fox Theater in Atlanta. That night Pauline dreamed she was Scarlet and Rhett Butler looked just like McLain Saranata.

August heat produced many air pockets in flight. It was a bad time for air travel because the passengers almost always got sick and used the comfort bags the whole time they were in the air. AM-23 made a scheduled run from Atlanta to Fort Worth but due to no passengers, the return am-22 passenger service was canceled. The DC-2 aircraft had to be ferried or flown back from Fort Worth to Atlanta empty with no passengers, but with the scheduled crew aboard that flight. The equipment, the DC-2 plane, was needed in Atlanta to originate another flight. As air travel increased, the airplanes were scheduled out on flights almost as soon as they landed at a destination.

Pauline was relieved on the return flight for it to be a ferry trip so she wouldn't have to take care of any more airsick passengers and to have the smell permeate the cabin in the August heat wave. She was gloating as she said to Mac, "I'm going to spend this whole trip with my feet propped up. I plan to read a magazine, stare out the window, and take a nap. You fellows just fly this bird home and let me vacation for a few hours."

Mac winked at Tommy conspiratorially. "Okay, Pauline. We'll give you a good ride."

Pauline awoke to feel herself straining against her seatbelt. The magazine she had been reading before she dozed off was floating toward the ceiling. Realizing they were in a dive, she immediately looked out the window to see if she could see a reason for the sudden motion. Seeing nothing, she mentally reviewed crash procedures Jean Cason had taught in stewardess school. Taking the pillow from behind her head, she started to fold her body around it when suddenly the plane was climbing. Pressed back against her seat, her confusion was magnified. *I never heard of a plane crashing upwards. What is going on?*

As the plane reached its apex of the climb, it nosedived again. Unfastened articles in the cabin were floating all about her as they passed through periods of zero gravity.

As the erratic flying continued, it began to dawn on her. He wouldn't! Surely he had more sense than to play games with company aircraft! He must think he's in a blooming air circus! When he finally regains his senses, I'm going to march into that cockpit and let him have it! She unbuckled her seatbelt and started toward the cockpit as the plane was climbing. Suddenly it took another nosedive and she felt her feet leave the aisle as she floated toward the ceiling. It was a breathtaking sensation. She felt like a feather, floating through air. About the time her head touched the ceiling, the plane began a steep climb, and she descended quickly.

She jumped into a passenger seat and fastened her seat belt tightly around her slim waist. The roller coaster ride continued and Pauline plotted her revenge. *I can't kill him because I don't want Tommy to have to fly back to Atlanta alone. I could pour the thermos of coffee on him but he would probably wear the dirty uniform and I'd have to look at it for a week. I could make him think I got hurt, or- hey- better still- I could possibly fool him into thinking that several passengers are mad as hornets and are going to sue.* Devious thoughts raced through her mind in her anxiety to get even with Mac for scaring her. *Yes, that is what I will do. He'll be so caught up in this devilment stunt flying, he won't realize for a minute that we don't have any passengers. I hope I can scare him as badly as he scared me. Why! I could have been killed! I'll get him for this. I'll pretend like he has passengers to answer to. It's a good thing he's a good pilot, otherwise, we'd all be cadavers. I should just go to the cockpit and regurgitate and let them live with the smell in this August heat. That would really get them! Course, then they would upchuck because it's like an epidemic- when one does it, everyone does it and then I'd be right back doing what I would have done had we had passengers on this flight.*

The plane leveled and stayed on a straight airway. Pauline cautiously unbuckled her seatbelt and stood, both hands holding onto something firm. She determinedly marched to the cockpit. With anger flashing, she charged, "What do you think you are doing? There are five hurt people in the cabin and three ready to sue the Southaire Corporation."

This was not what Mac expected to hear from her. He had been anticipating Pauline's arrival in the cockpit, but he thought she would come in laughing about his trick flying for her benefit.

Momentarily he was flabbergasted. "Oh, my lord! Are they hurt bad?" he started unbuckling his seatbelt to go check on the people. His face was ashen and he fumbled with the seat-belt in his haste.

Tommy innocently blurted, "What people? We have no passengers! This is a ferry trip!"

Mac's expression was worth all of Pauline's scheming. She slapped her thigh, tossed back her hair and laughed aloud.

"Hot damn, Pauline. You nearly scared the crap out of me! Oops, sorry, that slipped out!" he said as he eased back down into his captain's seat.

Sobering up, she parried, "Well, what do you think you did to me? I could have been injured or killed with your barnstorming!"

"Naw! I knew you'd be okay. I had Tommy check on you while youse was sleeping. We knowed you was fastened in."

They stared at each other for a few seconds until Tommy proclaimed, "Well, guess this takes care of this ferrying trip. What'll we do on the next one?"

Simultaneously they answered, "Oh shut up!"

Chapter 5—Amelia Earhart's Just Another Skirt

Women passengers were few in the early Forties. Passengers were mostly businessmen and they were often apprehensive about flying. Airline success or failure depended on the confidence and happiness businessmen experienced on each and every flight. Some of the first commercial travelers were people like Jay Gould and Will Rogers—people who liked doing exciting things and could afford air travel.

One day Amelia Earhart, noted woman aviatrix, boarded AM-23. Pauline was excited to have her as a passenger. Once in the air, Pauline took her to the cockpit door to introduce her to the pilots. Mac held the control wheel tightly, fearing all the while Lady Earhart might want to take over his airplane. He kept his gaze straight ahead and mumbled a disgruntled, "Hello, I'm busy." As the women were exiting, he glanced swiftly at Pauline and received her glare. *Whoops, she's mad at me. Well, cripes! I don't want that lady pilot in my cockpit. Women belong at home!*

Pauline was disgusted. Amelia Earhart was a brave woman, a pioneer and a famous passenger. With his rudeness, McLain had treated her like an ordinary woman, or even worse, not like a person at all.

At the first intermediate stop and as soon as they were away from passengers, the fight was on. "You are stupid, McLain. Rude and obnoxious! I was proud to introduce you as someone special and you acted like a clod!"

"No skirt is gonna call me names!"

"Skirt! That's all you know. Skirt, indeed! I'm glad this is our final crew rotation. I don't care to work with you another six months. I don't care to see you anymore, either. As a matter of fact, Tommy can serve you the rest of this trip and I hope you'll both be happy!"

"That suits me fine! I knew puttin' women on air-o-planes was a mistake and you're the biggest mistake of all. You ain't a woman! You're a smart aleck mouth!"

Southaire's gossip system vibrated with news of the argument. Mac and Pauline went their separate ways, flew opposite rotations and shrugged away gossip about each other from well- meaning co-workers.

The general offices of Southaire were expanded, more pilots and stewardesses were hired, and new DC-3 aircraft were being readied for service starting in the fast approaching year of 1941.

Pining of the wings was a special occasion when a new stewardess class graduated with six or seven girls in each class, and all Southaire personnel attended whenever possible. The class always looked so professional, dressed in white two-piece suits, with white gloves and military hats with gold wings on the front of them. They stood proudly on the stage as each had her flight stewardess wings pinned on the left lapel of the custom made hip-length jacket. Their skirts hung half-way down to their ankles and their chunky heeled white shoes completed the contemporary look of the Forties. They were all registered nurses in an enviable new career and they were anxious to get started.

The turnover rate among early stewardesses was high. Some found they didn't like to fly once they had made a few trips. Others got homesick and quit to go back home. Quite a few got proposals of marriage from their boyfriends because they found out they didn't like the idea of their girlfriends meeting so many exciting men. Very few lasted a year as stewardesses.

As Pauline watched the new graduating class receive their wings, she was remembering how thrilled she was when she graduated. Now she was very senior on the employment records. Almost all of her class had already quit flying.

With his heart nudging his Adam's apple, Mac approached Pauline when everyone stood to offer congratulations to the new class. He tentatively reached for her hand. "C'mon. I'll treat ya to a soda."

Her suppressed longing rose like a giant bubble in her throat, and her voice quivered with happiness as their hands met and their bodies strained toward each other. With a coquettish grin, she asked, "And a hot dog, too?"

"Oh lord, Pauline. All the hot dogs youse wants. Let's just get outta here."

"Oh yes, my captain." Her voice became husky. "You're in charge."

Oblivious to those surrounding them, Mac tucked her hand into the crook of his arm and placed his other trembling hand over it as he led Pauline from the room. Glances and grins followed their retreating backs by the Southaire family.

At Mac's car, he pulled her close. Pauline's response to his kiss surprised Mac so much that it wasn't until much later he realized she did not have on a corset.

On Christmas day of 1940, Mac presented Pauline with an engagement ring and the occasion was celebrated at a party at the Henry O'Grady that lasted ten hours.

In January, 1941, DC-3 service was inaugurated with Southaire Corporation offering 25-seat passenger flights. Both Mac and Pauline transferred to the new equipment. The passenger fare from Atlanta to Fort Worth was $38.50 and the trip took six hours at a speed of 165 miles per hour.

Tommy Jensen was promoted to a captain of the DC-2 aircraft, married his little brunette stewardess in a simple ceremony, and started flying with a copilot who cursed loudly whenever he had to pump the gear up, pump the flaps up and down, load the baggage, help work the meal forms, and take care of passengers when their stewardess wasn't feeling too well. Occasionally Tommy longed for his old AM-23 crew.

Competition was fierce between transportation companies. Stewardesses were definitely a part- a very important part- of the airline crew. Advertising was devoted to the *hostess on board.*

Pauline usually had loads of 21 passengers on DC-3s. Meal trays, silver, cloth napkins and beverages were packed separately. The full-course hot meats and vegetables were packed in thermal gallon jugs. Large soup ladles were used to dip food from containers.

In three minutes time, stewardesses were required to go to a passenger, place a pillow on his lap, ask what beverage he preferred (coffee, tea, or milk), return to the buffet, set up a complete tray service, return to the passenger, place the tray in his lap and do it all before the food got cold.

Each 90 mile leg of a flight took an hour and a half of work. In the buffet area, there were cold drawers for butter, cream, salad and dessert. There was storage for cups and trays. Hot water and coffee thermos jugs were mounted on top of buffet assembly space of 3 feet by 18 inches. Several times a copilot had to come back to help a stewardess complete her meal service on time.

Stewardesses on DC-3's had to have all the social graces and be a registered nurse, be a pioneer spokesman in the flying industry and be a public relations expert in encouraging passengers to continue flying on Southaire Corporation flights.

Scheduled for a 2030 (they had to use the 24 hour clock, so translated, 2030 was 8:30 p.m.) arrival in New Orleans, Mac landed DC-3 rotation, AM-57 on the runway at Jackson, Mississippi. He was informed by the radio tower that there was bad weather ahead and that New Orleans was socked in with zero visibility. Nothing was landing or taking off in the fog and mist surrounded the whole area. Before taxiing to the terminal, Mac called Pauline to the cockpit. "Tell your people we can't fly in to New Orleans tonight. Tell them we'll take them first thing in the morning as soon as the weather lets up. Tell them before they get off the plane. Otherwise, they might try for the Panama Limited. We don't want to lose any of those 21 men to a train. Bad business for our airline."

She winked. "I understand, captain. We won't lose our gentlemen passengers, sir."

She stepped to the front of the cabin. "Gentlemen, may I have your attention?" She was shouting above the din of propellers. "When we reach the terminal, please wait inside as a group. I will have an announcement regarding further flight preparations."

When the cabin door was opened, a ground personnel representative told her, "We have arranged for your passengers to stay at the Heidelberg Hotel. Southaire will take them into town, pay all their expenses, let them get a good night's rest and then continue this flight in the morning when the weather will let up."

Pauline knew it was her responsibility to keep the passengers content. To lose 21 to the Panama Limited would be a blow to the flying industry. It would not only hurt financially, it would hurt morale because it would shake confidence in flying. Twenty-one people talking about Southaire's inability to proceed as advertised would reach a lot of potential customers.

"A lot depends on you, Miss O'Shannon. Good luck!"

Like a mother hen, she gathered her brood. Using every ounce of her charm, Pauline convinced all 21 men to go on a special bus with her and airline representatives to the Hotel Heidelberg. After registering, the group gathered on the roof at the hotel's famous restaurant under the stars with a good dinner before them. They were pacified to a degree, but there was still that possibility they could change their minds about staying and catch the midnight Panama Limited into New Orleans that night.

What they needed was a good drink of liquor. But the Heidelberg Hotel was not licensed to serve drinks and it was dry as a bone. After dinner there was nothing Southaire could offer the passengers except a good nights rest and a continuing morning flight. As Pauline and Mac watched the men being served dinner, McLain wistfully declared "We ain't gonna keep 'em unless we can come by some booze."

"You're right, Mac. You hold them by your captain's authority as commander, even if you have to sing and dance or tell airline stories. I'll see what accommodations can be made available in the illegal beverage department." She excused herself and went to a telephone to call flight operations to ask for suggestions. One of the ground agents that had ridden in with them on the airline bus approached her. "Miss O'Shannon, Captain Saranata explained your problem. If you will allow me, I know a bootlegger out north of Jackson."

"Lead on. I am your copilot."

They drove through the night into dark woods, down a muddy overgrown pathway and stopped before a small hill. There was a door built into the side of the hill which led to an old storm cellar. After the Southaire ground agent kicked the door five quick times, the door opened a crack and a head appeared. The agent held up 3 fingers. In rapid succession, 3 brown gallon jugs were handed to the agent and Pauline. Money was swiftly taken and the door tightly closed. This was a harrowing night race to stem train popularity versus an airline that couldn't deliver. The 1940 roadster hurried with its two occupants and three jugs back to civilization- all for the cause of saving the airline.

Never had there been a party like the one on top of the Hotel Heidelberg by passengers of Southaire Corporation's AM-57! At a reasonable time the next morning 21 passengers were flown in flawless weather to New Orleans, and not one complaint was ever received about the overnight delay.

Chapter 6—Green Apples and Gastronomical Surgery

Pauline set their wedding date as March, 15, 1941, one year after she graduated from Southaire's first stewardess class. After marriage she planned to keep active by returning to school to work on her doctorate and resume a career in nursing as a superintendent, or to take flying lessons.

"You will do nothing of the kind. You will stay at home and raise da kids, my kids! And your kids, too!" McLain's chin jutted out and his mouth was drawn.

Pauline twirled a lock of his hair in her fingers. "McLain, I am not going to deny my potential. And don't try to inform me of my future limitations. I intend to make you aware, once and for all, that there are no limitations as to what I can do, or what you can do either, for that matter. First of all, it would be superb for you to also return to school and complete your education."

"Pauline, youse wait just a cotton-pickin minute. I might not object to youse going back to school for awhile, but I'll tell you like you said to me, once and fer ever, youse don't plan fer me and my doings."

With impish submission, she patted his cheek and said "Yes, dear". She knew all the time that she would have things her way.

On AM-14 rotation one blustery February evening, Pauline was reading aloud the weather report to her passengers while walking toward the cockpit when suddenly a Mr. Z. J. Carlson began gasping. As Pauline hurried to him, Carlson began to thrash about violently. Before she could do anything for him, the attack subsided. Beads of perspiration dotted his face and he attempted to loosen his three inch cellophane collar. Pauline quickly undid the studs freeing his expanded windpipe and two more shirt buttons, exposing grey hair curling over the edge of his BVDS. Leaving him breathing easier, she quickly got some cold water on a cloth and a cup of ice. Another spasm occurred and he doubled in agony.

Wiping his face and holding a chip of ice to his lips, Pauline commanded "Mr. Carlson! Mr. Carlson! Please try to tell me the location of your pain. I am a nurse. I want to help you! Please lie back in your seat and let me assist you. I have medication but I must know what is wrong."

"It's my stomach. It feels like I am being stabbed."

"Will you let me feel, sir? Just let me check your right side."

He eyed her suspiciously. Then, when another spasm racked his perspiring body, he shouted, "Yes! Yes! Help me!"

Pauline knowledgeably reached fingertips near his appendix and began to press. There was no reaction. His abdomen felt taut, but he did not respond to pressure about his appendix.

"Mr. Carlson, I don't believe you are experiencing an appendicitis attack. Have you eaten anything recently you know of which might give you a stomach ache? Maybe a green apple?"

"No, no! It isn't a belly ache. I've had those. This is different. It's a stabbing pain! No, I haven't eaten any green apples. Get me a doctor."

"Hold this ice to your lips."

She stood up and called loudly. "Is anyone on board a physician? We have an ill passenger."

Several shook their heads. She went forward to the cockpit. "Mac, you had better radio ahead for a doctor. Passenger Z. J. Carlson is experiencing abdominal pain."

"Is it appendicitis?"

"I don't believe so. I think it's something else. I'm going to try to examine him further."

"Do you need help?"

"No."

She returned to Carlson who was again in agony with spasms, thrashing and groaning.

A lady across the aisle started crying. "He's going to die. He's going to die."

Pauline removed the lady's hands from her weeping face and then whispered 'Shush! He must have quiet and rest. He is not going to die. Please don't cry. You'll only upset Mr. Carlson."

The pain subsided and the exhausted man laid his head against the cool windowpane. Pauline again felt his appendix area carefully. With no indication of sensitivity, she spoke softly. "Mr. Carlson, I'm going to give you some paregoric in warm water. I'm not positive, but I believe you are experiencing gallstone colic. A doctor has been notified and will meet our flight. The paregoric will ease your pain. We'll be landing in about 45 minutes. Please try to relax."

Pauline removed paregoric from her medical kit, measured two teaspoons of the amber liquid into a cup and filled it half full with warm water. He drank it while watching her with trusting eyes. When the next spasm came, his confidence in her waned and he looked worried again.

She patted his arm and wiped his face with a cold, wet cloth. "It will take a few minutes for the paregoric to ease your pain. Please try to relax."

Soon he was dozing.

A week later, in the midst of bridal preparations, Pauline received a call from Jean Canons, Southaire's chief stewardess.

"Your passenger on AM-14 on February 26, Z. J. Carlson, sent a letter to Mr. A. F. Williams. He asked you be notified that he did have gallstones. He is in the hospital recovering from surgery, but his secretary has instructions to bring you the largest box of chocolates money can buy. He wanted the president of Southaire to know about your extra service aboard your flight and wants to have the candy personally delivered by his secretary."

"Wow! I didn't expect anything. I hope Mr. Carlson is progressing satisfactorily. It would be nice to have the candy delivered to your office Jean, and then everyone can enjoy it. I'd like to share the chocolates with fellow workers and I happen to know Jacob's Confectionery Store has a whopping special occasion 25 pound box for sale. You might mention this to Mr. Carlson's secretary when you tell her where to bring it."

"You don't miss much, do you Pauline?

Pauline chuckled and answered, "Well, Jean, I had you for an instructor, didn't I?"

"How are wedding plans coming? Still going to hogtie McLain?"

"Oh my heavens yes, Jean. There's a whole new world available to Mac that he doesn't know exists, and I intend to introduce him to it. If he thought adding a *skirt to his air-o-plane* meant changes, just wait until he marries me!"

The Fifties

Be an airline stewardess!

Join America's most interesting profession for young women who qualify. Travel . . . good pay . . . interesting work . . . fly 85 hours month . . . training takes place in Atlanta, Georgia, home office of the Southaire Corporation . . . train in six weeks . . . no cost to trainee . . . receive $120.00 expense money during training . . . lodging and meals furnished.

Stewardesses are paid a base salary

Plus flight pay which varies with the type of airplane they fly. For example, a stewardess flying 85 hours on a Convair would start at $240.00 per month. The ability to speak a foreign language is not required unless a stewardess flies international flights.

   Basic requirements are:

   ✦ A minimum of two years college . . . single, never
      have been married . . . unimpaired vision (glasses
      or contact lenses not permissible) . . . clear com-
      plexion . . .attractive . . .even white teeth . . .neat
      appearance . . .pleasing personality . . .high moral
      character . . .good physical condition . . .and must
      pass an entrance examination, complete physical
      and periodic examinations.
   ✦ You must be 21 to 26 years of age, 5' 1 1/2" to
      5' 6 1/2" in height, with weight in proportion to
      height, and a maximum weight of 125 pounds.

   If you meet our qualifications, we will arrange a personal interview with you.

On May 1, 1953, Chiwest Airlines formally merged with and into the Southaire Corporation. This brought to Southaire a route system of 5,854 miles, serving 22 domestic cities and 6 foreign countries, making Southaire an international airline. There was a greater need for stewardesses, including girls who could speak Spanish and fly overseas rotations. Mothers and fathers were hesitant about daughters traveling out of the United States. They were still getting used to their daughters having careers in the sky.

Fidel Castro was assembling his first band of guerrillas.

Chapter 7—Convair who?

John Saterfield, superintendent of passenger service, was interviewing. With fingertips pressed together and intense concentration, he inquired of the ex-cheerleader before him, "Why do you want to be a Southaire stewardess?"

Penny Perkins tossed her thick auburn tresses and unleashed her thoughts. "It'll be a great, wonderful life. The salary is terrific. I'll meet new people and see the world. It's the thing to do for today's woman and tomorrow's leaders. I'll wear good looking uniforms. I'll get to date movie stars, have fabulous vacations, marvelous . . ."

"Wait!" Saterfield raised his hand. "Miss Perkins, do you know what a Convair is?"

"Uh, Mr. Saterfield, I have to be honest. I don't know a Convair from a rocking chair. But I sure am willing to learn. I'm a fast learner and, as you know from my application, I made good grades at Texas Tech. It'll only take me one trip on a Convair to know all about them."

Class began at 0800 on Monday. Penny was one of a dozen trainees, and per instructions in the letters of acceptance, they were similarly dressed- skirt, blouse, bra and girdle with silk stockings with seams attached to the girdle, and high heels.

Lorna Hodges, Miss Fashion herself, instructor, and self-confirmed bachelorette, greeted the young ladies.

"First of all, we'll start with rules and regulations. You will be taught every phase of being with an airline, except actual flying maneuvers. And when we are through, you will feel qualified to take over the cockpit. These next six weeks you belong to us. You will do homework every night and on weekends. You will take observation flights and then make reports on them. During your last two weeks of training, you will be all over the airplane and busier than you can imagine. You will have no dates, no social life during your training. Yes, you heard me correctly. No dates, no fun, just a lot of hard work—and yes that does seem mean. You have a tremendous amount of memorizing to do, and you will concentrate on being a stewardess, because once you graduate, you are on your own."

She walked past the seats looking at each girl. "You will not have a chance to ask for help when in doubt on the airplane, so it is important that you learn everything now. Then, in case of emergency, you will automatically know what to do. After you leave this classroom at the end of six weeks, you will be responsible for the lives and for the comfort of as many as sixty people at one time. It won't be easy, but it will be worth the torture that we are going to put you through. Are there any questions or resignations before we begin?"

Penny turned to Jane, one of her roommates at the boarding house and whispered. "Sixty people! Wow! That's a lot of lunches."

The first day was full of general company policies, procedures and discussions of things they were to study in weeks ahead. They were in class from eight to five with an hour lunch period, two coffee breaks and two five minute smoking periods. They were being initiated into the Southaire family.

At the boarding house selected by Southaire, lights were turned off promptly at 10 p.m. Penny was in the process of writing to special boyfriend, Jody, back in Lubbock, Texas when the lights went out and she suddenly realized that the curfew rule was strict with no exceptions.

During the initial week, they were given their hardest homework, memorizing the complete flying routes of all Southaire flights. At the end of training they were told they would be given a final examination during which they had to draw a map showing every flight, every stop and the kind of equipment that was used.

The days passed swiftly with discussions about the use of all emergency equipment, weekly tests and lessons in first aid. They were even briefed in the possibility that they might have to deliver a baby. Every weekend, dressed in hats, suits and gloves, they posed as passengers, took flights to and from different cities and watched the stewardesses at work. They wrote their observations of the activities, turned them in on Mondays, were graded and reprimanded if they missed certain things that they were supposed to notice.

During the third week, they were measured for uniforms, and bought shoes, blouses and handbags. The uniforms were tailor-made and as Penny put on a sample uniform from which measurements were taken, she felt a tingle travel down her spine as she thought about the day when she would wear this uniform.

They were given instructions in the subtle use of make-up, complete with the use of eye shadow and the forming of a more perfect lip line. They had their hair styled. It if was too long, it was cut short. If it was bleached, it was restored to its natural color. They were advised about shades of nail polish and hosiery. They were taught how to cover up a blemish or scar on their faces if there was one, no matter how tiny. They were subjected to complete physical examinations.

The fourth and fifth weeks they spent on the airplanes in the hangers, using the emergency exits, ropes and slides. They were taken through airplanes that were torn apart to be checked. On these planes they were asked many questions about the heating systems, air vents, oxygen outlets, emergency lights and cockpit exits. They were asked the same questions over and over. Any girl that made a mistake or got mixed up on her answers was taken back through the plane and had each piece of equipment explained to her again. The others could not just stand and watch. They had to make the trip back with her and instructor Hodges in turn would ask them the same questions over and over.

Everything was drilled into their heads so that they would be able to put their hands on anything they needed in complete darkness within just a matter of seconds. They crawled on the wings, jumped off into a mechanic's waiting arms and climbed up and down the emergency ropes until they had blisters on their delicate hands. They were timed as they took turns evacuating the airplane of practice passengers by using all the emergency procedures that they were supposed to have learned. They spent considerable time watching the mechanics put the airplanes back together and they learned the names and functions of many of the parts.

One day Loran Hodges told them they were in for a surprise. They were led by Loran to a seaplane on the ramp and told to board it. Soon after they were seated, the engines began warming and in just a few minutes they were airborne. They watched out the window as the plane flew across the city and to a large lake. They had been flying with unanswered curiosity when at last Loran made an announcement. "We're going to simulate a crash landing and evacuation. Fasten your seat belts, remove all sharp objects, lean forward, grasp your arms behind your knees and assume crash position. When we hit the water, get the life rafts, and assist each other off the airplane. You only have seconds to do this, so make each movement mean something. After you are out of the plane and in the life raft, give distress signals and practice first aid on each other. We will spend the remainder of the day in the water. Now get ready."

Penny lamented to Jane, "In the water! And I've got on my new Capezio shoes. I'll just die if they get ruined."

The class survived, but they wondered if they were going to be exposed to any more such treatment. Wet and disheveled, they were returned to the airport in Atlanta. Loran instructed them, "Tonight write a thorough report of today's activities that could be submitted to the C.A.B. (Civil Air Board) pending a full investigation. Tell them exactly what you did in this situation."

Penny concluded her twice weekly letter to Jody. *Honey, I can make my report short and sweet—we was dunked! I'm tempted to write that in my C.A.B. report, but you and I both know I have more sense than to do something that crazy. After all, I fell in love with you three years ago and that proves how much sense I really have. Nite, my darling.*

Evenings, the trainees studied, memorized homework, recited to each other and fell into bed exhausted, sometimes before the 10 p.m. curfew. They began to think this was the longest six weeks of their life.

The final week they were groomed and in their new uniforms, given another physical and briefed for the final exam. They served meals to each other, made practice public address system announcements, walked on a moving belt on a mock airplane and served each other as though passengers.

On Wednesday they were given their final examination which took eight hours and were graded before they were dismissed for the day. One of the girls failed her final examination and was terminated from Southaire. Thursday was declared a day off to rest and write letters, to do shopping and to have their hair styled.

On Friday at 0900, they gathered in the classroom and listened to speeches of congratulations, and heard what was expected of them as representatives of Southaire airlines. Then their wings were pinned on at a luncheon celebration and they received their diplomas. The public saw them for the first time in their new uniforms. Penny felt as if her heartbeat was showing right through the shiny gabardine material.

Chapter 8—The Meals are
for Passengers

After getting moved from the boarding house into an apartment near the airport with Jane and two other classmates, Penny was eager for her first flight. It was a 'hurry up and wait' situation. She was on reserve.

Being lowest on the seniority scale, reserve meant she had no scheduled assignments and was on call for 24 hours at a time. She had to be primped and polished and ready to go if a phone call from crew scheduling told her to report.

Waiting impatiently for her first chance to be a stewardess was frustrating. Imprisoned in the apartment, Penny rearranged her drawers three times, polished all her shoes and changed her hair style twice. She decided to treat her roommates to a Texas style chocolate cake and had just slipped the pans into the oven when the phone rang.

"Yes. This is she. Yes, I'll be right there. Oh, yes, sir. I'll hurry. I'm leaving now. Bye. Oh, thank you for calling me. Okay, I'm on my way. Bye again.'

Hanging up, she immediately called a cab. Penny raced through the apartment, jumped into her uniform, snatched up her hat, rearranged her hairdo with a quick brushing, stuffed her bulging make-up kit into her overnight bag, and with a final grab, slung her purse strap over her shoulder. Pausing briefly in front of the full length mirror, she checked to see that the lace on the bottom of her blouse slip didn't show and that the dark seams of her hose were straight. Rushing out the door just as the horn announced the arrival of the taxi, she left her special cake to char in the oven. It was found two hours later by a roommate who smelled it.

After checking in with operations, Penny boarded the shiny new Convair 304 to which she was assigned. She felt a wave of stage fright as she looked down the rows of empty seats that would soon be filled with passengers that would be her sole responsibility. But as the remembered telling Mr. Saterfield back in her interview, "One trip aboard a Convair and I'll know it all."

The caterer came to her and handed her a clipboard. "The meals are on board. Sign for 'em."

"Not until I check them."

In a few minutes Penny was standing in the entrance way of the small ship ready to greet her first passengers. The first man aboard was lugging a bulging briefcase and appeared involved with his own business worries.

"Good day, sir. I'm Penny Perkins. This is my first flight but don't look so worried because you'll have a great flight. I'll do everything to make this an enjoyable trip. We have new issues of all magazines and the coffee is piping hot. It's a beautiful day and . . ."

"Excuse me, miss," he interrupted. "Do you mind if I take my seat? There are a lot of people behind me."

A flustered Penny bid the rest of her passengers no more than a cheery "Hello."

Immediately involved in takeoff preparations, she worked on the seat chart between hanging wraps and checking personal belongings in the overhead rack. She was about half-way through getting passenger names and destinations when the agent brought the takeoff paperwork. Scanning the weather print-out, she quickly took the clearance and computer sheet to the cockpit.

With an assertive nod to her crew in answer to their "You ready?" Penny made her way to the rear of the Convair, checking seat belts along the way. As she lifted the microphone for her first 'welcome aboard' public announcement, she felt the plane begin to taxi.

Exhilaration and anticipation of takeoff pushed her into the speech before she had time to gather her scattered thoughts. "Ladies and gentlemen, we are landing at Charleston. It has been our pleasure to have you aboard Southaire. Please check for all personal items before you leave your seat. Please plan to make you next trip aboard another Southaire flight. Have a happy day."

Pleased that she had made it through her memorized speech, Penny buckled herself into the jump seat in the buffet area and smiled at the few passengers who turned around to stare at her during takeoff.

As soon as the seat belt sign went off, Penny hopped to her feet, gathered an armful of magazines and started to pass them in the cabin. The first man she approached had on a navy uniform and a wide grin covered his crew-cut, youthful expression. "That was a mighty short trip, ma'am."

"Huh?"

"You just said we were landing in Charleston."

"Oh, my gosh! I did, didn't I?"

She looked around the cabin quickly and felt every eye was on her. "Oh, how stupid! I could kill myself. I'm gonna die right here. I've got to get back on the P.A. and straighten this out right now before I do another thing. Here. Hold these magazines."

Flustered and embarrassed, Penny clicked on the P.A. "Golly, I'm sorry. I guess I made a mistake. We're not really landing. But we're going to . . . in a little while . . . we really are. But first, I have to welcome you aboard. Uh, just a minute . . . ladies and gentlemen, welcome aboard Southaire's flight 247 to Charleston. Our approximate arrival time will be 12:56. We will be flying at an altitude of 14,000 feet and cruising at a ground speed of 320 miles per hour."

Penny completed the standard welcome speech and then compulsively chattered on.

"Many of you probably know by now this is my first flight as a Southaire stewardess. But I want you to know I am well trained to make you comfortable and to handle any emergency situations like a fire or crash, of if the pilot had a heart attack. But ooops, I don't mean I can fly this plane . . . just forget all about that emergency stuff . . . I shouldn't say all that. It isn't gonna happen. Why Southaire has the best safety record of any airline today."

She went on to tell her amused passengers, "That's one of the reasons I chose Southaire to fly with. I came straight from college into this job."

She ended her speech when she heard a restless child crying near the rear. Penny took the child's hand and led her up to the front of the plane and reached into her flight kit. She pinned on a pair of junior stewardess wings. "Now I need you to help me count all the people. You are my assistant. Next you can help me pass out magazines and pillows." Before they worked their way to the back, two more restless youngsters insisted they also get wings and be helpers.

When the seat belt sign came on in preparation for landing, Penny had a hard time getting her miniature co-helpers to sit with their mothers. She had to convince them there was room for only one on the stewardess jump seat in the buffet area. Penny repeated her landing speech buckled into the jump seat near the public announcement system as the wheels touched down on the runway at Charleston.

After she had seen her last passenger deplane, the Captain came back into the cabin. She was proud of the fine job she had done and knew she was on her way to becoming an excellent stewardess and a fine representative of Southaire.

The Captain inquired, "Well, Miss Perkins, how did it go?"

Bubbling, she answered. "Not a single problem! I'm sure flying will agree with me."

"Did you have any trouble with your quick meal service? A lot of the girls do, especially new gals."

Penny stared, her eyes opening wide in horror.

"Oh, golly mollies! I forgot all about the meal service. I didn't serve those people a thing. I only talked to them. What do you suppose will happen? I was so nervous that I just talked. I guess I talked myself out of a job. I could just die!"

"Well now, child, don't worry about it. If that was the worst thing that ever happened on this airline, everyone would be shouting. I doubt that you will be fired. We'll just eat all we want to and we'll share the rest of the meals with the cargo men and agents. I can eat three trays of food myself. Now don't worry your pretty head."

Penny didn't get fired, but a few days latter there was a note in her stewardess mailbox reminding her that meals were for passengers and the public address system was only for interesting comments or emergency use.

Jody placed a rare long distance call from Lubbock to see how things were going with Penny. As soon as she heard his voice, she began a non-stop recap of her experiences of her first flight. Despite the minor problems encountered, she was enthusiastic about her job and was looking forward to future flights. She went on at length about that nice captain who helped her out with the problem with the meal service.

"Jody, I'm sure he's the reason I didn't get fired. He's just the sweetest man and he wrote a real nice report about me. I sure hope I get to fly with him again soon."

"Penny! I didn't spend my money to hear you rave about some other guy!"

"Oh, honey, you know it's you I love. He's old enough to be my uncle."

The operator's metallic voice interrupted. "Your three minutes are up."

"Penny, gotta go. Got no more dough with me. Write me a long letter."

Chapter 9—We're Landing
at the Airport

Within 24 hours, crew scheduling had called Penny for another flight. This time it was a DC-6 with another, more senior stewardess, on a turn-around to New Orleans. The senior stewardess made a flawless take-off speech, guided Penny through the meal service and in-flight chores without mishap. But it fell to Penny to make the approach public announcement speech into New Orleans. Rattled from her two hours of constant activity, she proved that she had not yet mastered public announcement techniques when she picked up the microphone and said, "Ladies and gentlemen, we are landing at . . . uh, the, uh, uh, the, ladies and gentlemen, we are landing in just a few minutes at . . .uh, the, uh . . .oh, darn, . . .we are landing at the airport!"

One smart passenger shouted, "For awhile there, I thought we would land before she finished."

Being junior in seniority on the flight, Penny remained on board the empty plane to straighten magazines and replace pillows in the overhead rack. Satisfied the plane was in order, she went to join her crew in operations. As she opened the door, she heard the senior stewardess' voice. "She even botched up the approach announcement. Personnel sure lets a kook slip through once in awhile." Her voice trailed off as she noticed Penny at the door. "Here she is now, our little reserve gal. Hi Penny. Come on over." She turned back to the co-pilot with whom she had been conversing. "As I was just saying, this girl certainly has great potential."

Penny had just finished polishing her nails when crew scheduling called two days later. "Miss Perkins, one of the stews scheduled for a charter just sprained her ankle. The charter is to Las Vegas. It's a group of 65 air conditioner sales managers on a constellation aircraft. Miss

Maxwell will be senior stew. You'll be gone about 36 hours."

"When do you want me at the airport?" Penny interrupted. "All I have to do is get dressed, and pack my bag, and fix my hair, and call a cab, and I can be there in just a little while. Oh yes, I also have to write a note to . . ."

"Okay, Miss Perkins, no big rush. You've got a couple of hours. The flight leaves at 1310. It's going to be a lot different from the flights you've been on before. Do you think you can handle it?"

"Oh yes, sir, I won't have any trouble. I've learned so much from my previous flights. I know nothing is going to happen that I can't handle. Besides, I know I'll get along fine with the passengers. I just love air conditioning!"

"Yeah, sure, Miss Perkins. You're going to have a real interesting flight. And so are those salesmen."

"Oh yes, sir. I'll do everything I . . ."

"Why don't you come out a little early so the senior stew, Miss Maxwell, can meet you and can brief you on what to expect."

"Thank you for calling. I'm so excited. I've never been to Las Vegas before. I wonder what the weather . . ." She stopped when she realized that the gentleman in crew scheduling must have been cut off.

Gayle Maxwell briefed Penny in the stewardess lounge as they gathered flight report blanks, cleaning certificates for spillage accidents, and medical forms. "A charter is a much freer sort of flight, Penny. We have no scheduled duties. We just play it by ear. There will be a bar and then men can help themselves or we can serve them."

"I don't know very much about mixing cocktails, but I can learn. I'm a fast learner."

"Don't worry, dear, you'll get more help than you need. To our passengers this will be one big party. They all know each other and will be a lot more relaxed. They'll play jokes on you, try to get you to drink and play cards with them and flirt outrageously."

When the men were boarded, it took the two stewardesses fifteen minutes to convince the salesmen of the necessity of fastening their seat belts, even on charters.

Penny had to convince one persuasive passenger that she absolutely could not share his seat and seat belt with him. Mentally she hoped to remember to tell Gayle to beware of this one. She leaned over to read his name badge—Harry Lawson—and withdrew quickly from his reaching hand.

The minute the seat belt sign went off in the air, the cabin erupted into activity. Shouts of "open the bar" snowballed into a chant, accompanied by clapping hands and whistling. Gayle manned the bar as Penny prepared hors d'oeuvres in the buffet area.

Meeting in the center aisle, Gayle passing drinks and Penny holding a tray of food, Penny muttered, "It's just like one great big kindergarten class."

Gayle replied as she swooped to keep her tray balanced as two men grabbed for drinks off it, "You ain't seen nothing yet."

Several round of drinks later, Penny was trying to persuade some of the passengers into trying a less potent beverage. "Coffee, fellows, coffee or juice?"

She approached one unusually quiet young man and saw that he was trying to hide his nervousness behind the large pages of Life magazine.

'First ride?"

"Yes it is."

"There's nothing to worry about."

"Yes."

"Would you like coffee or juice?"

"Yes."

"Yes, what?"

"Yes, ma'am!"

"I meant, oh, just a minute. I'll be right back."

Returning with two glasses of orange juice, she eased into the vacant seat beside him and handed him his drink, then took a sip of the other one. "Flying is a lot of fun when you get used to it."

"It's not so bad so far, but I don't like the bumps. They make me think the plane is falling out of the sky."

"Ah, yes—the air pockets. They are scary. They're part of flying. Turbulence is caused when we encounter a difference in air pressure, but they're no danger whatsoever. You go over bumps when you drive your car. Just think of air pockets as large chuckholes in the road."

"It always seemed like going through the air would be smooth."

"The airfoil or teardrop shape of this plane is designed to get a reaction from the flow of air and produce maximum stability. But when we encounter changing barometric pressure in cumulus or nimbostratus clouds, we catch a downdraft and it is frightening. But please don't worry. You should be having the time of your life on this trip."

"I feel better after talking to you."

"Penny, come help!" Gayle called from the middle of a cloud of feathers surrounding a heated pillow fight.

After they got the men settled down a bit, Penny started serving coffee to the feathery opponents. She was serving the last one when she saw a grey flannel covered arm reaching toward the air vent with a steaming cup of coffee. She moved quickly to stop him, but she was too late. The high pressured jet of air emptied the cup, saturating the man, sobering him into sputtering and dripping wretchedness.

"I was just trying to cool it off."

"Are you alright? Did you get burned?"

"No. It cooled it off alright." He licked a droplet off his upper lip.

"I'll get you a towel."

Infectious laughter filling the area caught up with Penny and she began giggling as she noticed the coffee splattered lettering on his name tag. "Your hands keep getting you in trouble, Mr. Harry Lawson."

"You better believe it, honey." He made a grab for her.

They arrived in Las Vegas raring to go, determined not to miss a sight, and bound to get the most out of every cent they brought with them.

As they deplaned, with reminders of departure time from the two stewardesses at the door, fast-handed Harry Lawson grabbed Miss Maxwell by the wrist. "We can't do this town right without our two charming hostesses. Somebody grab little copper Penny and let's go."

As Gayle was being swept down the steps, Penny looked around helplessly. The pilot and copilots approached the exit as a couple of the passengers halted traffic to echo Harry's invitation.

"C'mon, we want you to join us. Seriously, be our guests." The men turned to the three pilots. "You too! C'mon, let's go!"

Captain Huber said, 'Sounds like fun. Come on, girls, let's join these gentlemen and see the sights of Vegas."

As they walked across the tarmac, Penny bubbled to the young man who had worried about air pockets, "I'm so excited. I've never gambled before. Do you think I'll win something?"

He smiled down at her. "I've calculated a system. Stick with me and I'll guarantee you'll win some money."

Penny and Gayle trudged into their hotel room after being in the gaming halls all night. They flung themselves into bed not bothering to fully undress. Each had been moderately successful at their first venture into the gambling casinos.

Preparing to return home, the only thing bright and shiny was the airplane. The girls were still tired and the men were downright funereal.

Deplaning at charter's end in Atlanta, the stewardesses trudged homeward as the bright glare of another morning sun aggravated their lingering headaches.

A few days later after another flight, Penny remarked "Jane, you'll never guess who I had on board." Without waiting for Jane to venture an answer, Penny beamed. "James Stewart, that's who! He is the nicest person and looks just like he does on the movie screen. He talked to us and to some of the passengers. And guess what? "She cocked her head to one side in a superior manner." He drinks his coffee just like I do—with gobs of milk. He was so friendly. Just think, Jane, a real honest to goodness movie star was on my flight today. When he got off, he told us that he had a very nice trip and I reached out and he shook my hand. Want to take a picture of my hand, the one shook by Mr. Jimmy Stewart?"

"No you goose! I don't want to take a picture of your hand. I had Phyllis Kirk on my last trip. She didn't say much but she had all the men goggle-eyed. Wonder how I would look with my hair fixed like hers, straight bangs and shoulder pageboy?" Jane crossed to stand in front of the apartment full length mirror.

Penny watched her roommate primp and push at her brownish short hair. "You can't 'cause Southaire won't let you wear your hair touching your collar, unless you wear a hairnet. Say, Jane, you can get a wig."

"No I can't. They are too expensive. Besides, the only people that wear wigs are people in show business. Southaire would never approve a wig."

Just when Penny had despaired of its ever coming, autumn arrived. The muggy heat lifted from the city, nudged on its way by crisp breezes. The transformation coaxed the girls from their summer doldrums and created the urge to go shopping for fall clothes.

The winds sent bits of paper and occasional leaves from city bound trees on a frantic race down Peachtree Street. Jane and Penny clutched their jackets around them against the brisk chill and gazed into the colorful store windows. Frozen images of fantasy women smiled from the display windows.

"Look at that sweater set!" exclaimed Penny, shielding her hat from the assault of an airborne newspaper. "The blue one there, on the mannequin that looks like Rhonda Fleming. C'mon lets go in here."

They ducked inside the warm brightness of Rich's department store to browse. Shopping until closing time, they emerged into the fading dusk, tired and burdened with parcels. The street lights competed for attention with a brilliant moon playing hide and seek among the wind-shredded clouds. A faint whiff of burning leaves mingled with the dinner time smells of Atlanta's restaurants as the two stewardesses hurried back to their apartment.

Penny and Jane and their class gained seniority as other stewardesses classes graduated behind them. They had regular rotations and occasionally flew together for a month when bids coincided.

Chapter 10—Poker Chips and Boarding Passes

A cold, dark night with lousy TV programming prompted Penny to suggest, "Let's invite the pilots from next door over for some penny poker and popcorn."

Her roommates agreed. It was one of those rare occasions when they were all in the apartment together. Brenda went to fetch their neighbors while Jane started popping corn. Narda cleared an area in the middle of the living room carpet, pitched down a few toss pillows from their sofa and scattered ashtrays about.

Penny got a huge pickle jar of coins which the roomies used as a common fun-money bank. She grabbed a new deck of Southaire playing cards which Narda had taken from an airplane and broke the seal.

Neighbors, popcorn, cokes, pillows, ashtrays, money and cards filled the center of the carpet when the game began at 8 p.m. At first the four roommate hostesses were dominating the game despite the efforts of the two pilots from the next apartment.

At 2300 (11 p.m.), just as he was beginning to recoup his losses, one of the pilots had to leave for a Cincinnati flight. Just before midnight there was a knock at the door. In came a fellow stewardess who lived across the courtyard and her date. They explained that they had seen the lights on and were in need of a place to share a nightcap because her roommates were already asleep.

"Hey, wow!" he exclaimed as they saw the game in progress.

Jane yelled from the floor. "Pull up a cushion and join us."

"Deal us in." He was already pulling off his suit coat.

With the new players, the original refreshments were depleted. Jane withdrew from the game for a few minutes to pop some more corn. Ever the good neighbor, the remaining pilot went home for more beer and cokes.

The players were so involved with the competition in the game that Brenda's wave, as she succumbed to sleep and stumbled off to the bedroom, was barely acknowledged.

After a throw-together breakfast served picnic style on the floor, the pilot again proved a good neighbor by offering the young man who had come in with the date his shaving equipment and a refreshing shower. His exclamation of "Oh my gosh! I'm due at my office in an hour!" threw the game into a temporary hiatus while everyone scurried to ready him for his junior executive position in an accounting firm. Penny brushed off his coat, his date offered to press his trousers, but he declined her offer, and after shaving next door at the pilot's apartment, he bid them all farewell.

After giving her departing date a goodbye kiss, the stewardess from across the courtyard unpinned and shook free her sleek French twist hairstyle. "Ah, much better. I was beginning to get a headache. Who's dealing?"

Two more neighboring pilots, returning from trips, heard the laughter from the girls' apartment and poked their heads inside. Seeing the game, they inquired, "Want some fresh money?" A chorus of "You bet we do" greeted them. They dropped their flight bags just inside the door, peeled off uniform jackets, hats and ties and asked for black coffee as they sank to the floor.

Sam returning from Cincinnati at noon, heard the game still going on, and entered without knocking. They promptly sent him for hamburgers, malts and French fries. Brenda woke and joined them for hamburgers, replacing Penny who finally gave up the fight to keep her eyes open and went to bed after eating.

The game continued its player shuffle as the stewardess from across the courtyard left to get some sleep and sent one of her roommates back as a replacement. Sam's roommate and the only original male in the game left reluctantly to catch needed winks before going out on a flight to Charlotte. Taking his winnings with him, it was evident how he had come by the nickname "dealer".

The day was everything the night before had promised—grey, cold and damp. Clouds marched across the sky shifting positions even more often than the participants in the rotating poker game in apartment B-7. Another victim succumbed. Jane gave up about 1800 and went to bed.

After twenty-four hours of hard poker playing, with an occasional cat-nap with her head up against the sofa arm, Narda began preparing to go to work. She showered, took a caffeine tablet and put on her uniform and coat. Flinching at the blast of smoke-free air when she opened the front door, she departed to take out her fatigue on her helpless passengers.

When Penny returned to the arena just before midnight, one of the pilots was bidding everyone goodbye. He picked up his flight bag from the doorway and shrugged-off farewell shouts of "Chicken! Can't take it! Quitter!"

Penny's hunger pains prompted her to begin cajoling Sam into loaning her his car. "Come on Sam, I'm starving and I don't want breakfast food. I want pizza—hot, spicy pizza. It's too far to walk. I'll bring you some too. I'll bring some for everybody! Just give me your keys! She started punching him. "Awhooooo, awhooooo."

He handed over his keys and rolled his eyes in silent prayer for the safety of his new T-bird. Before they could grab her, Penny scooped up the money in the pot, shouted, "Dutch treat, gang," and was out the door.

Jane heard the cheering when Penny returned with three large pepperoni pizzas and came into the living room for her share.

Penny shivered. "Boy, it's cold outside. That rain feels like it's gonna turn to snow."

"Good poker playing weather!" Sam snatched his keys from her hand and pocketed them.

The quitter who left earlier returned about dawn, refreshed after a few hours sleep. "I'm the only one around here with any sense. Now get ready to have your pockets cleaned out."

They played constantly for four days and nights with the number of players ranging from five to nine at varying times. Each participant left the game at least once to "keep 'em flying", then returned.

When the marathon poker game finally broke up, the bleary eyed guests went out to face blazing sunshine and balmy breezes. Typical of Atlanta's unpredictable climate, the weather had changed from a premature winter to a mock Indian summer. The bare trees seemed out of place in the almost tropical warmth and the players felt foolish carrying their heavy coats. But the balmy days were only a short interlude before the biting cold and rain-saturated winter in Georgia.

Having a few days off, Penny took advantage of her earned half-fare ticket plan and splurged on a round trip home to Texas. She couldn't bear the idea of a gloomy Thanksgiving alone in Atlanta when her parents, fiancée, and surely better weather awaited her in Lubbock.

Jody met her at the airport. "Penny, I'm not letting you go back. I've missed you so much. Let's not wait the year we promised your folks. Let's go to Carlsbad, New Mexico right now and find a justice of the peace and get married today."

"Jody, honey, don't be silly. You know good and well we're gonna have a church wedding. We both agreed that the future Mrs. Joseph Stinsen is going to be educated and well traveled. Quit being impetuous and quit kissing me like that. I wanna go see my folks. They're waiting on us. C'mon, start this buggy. I'll bet my lipstick's smeared to kingdom come."

"I'm gonna smear it more than that tonight!"

Her five day holiday went by in a blur of activities, visits with old friends, a fraternity dance, and long conversations with Jody. He repeatedly tried to persuade her to quit her job and settle down at the ranch with him.

"Jody! Honey! I can't! I'm not ready yet." As she got on the plane with one last promise to Jody to think about it, she realized that despite all her explaining, he still didn't understand her need to do something on her own before she settled down to life as a rancher's wife in the West.

On her next working flight, a young widow accompanying her husband's body home to Atlanta from Florida upset Penny. During the flight, most of which Penny spent lending a sympathetic ear to the bereaved girl, Penny learned that the young man had been killed in one of those freak auto accidents where the wife sitting next to him was barely scratched. They were on their way to Miami for an eagerly anticipated vacation.

Penny was touched by the pathetic young widow and did all she could to make the flight as comfortable as possible. Seeing how the plans of a young marriage could be terminated so quickly made Penny think about herself and Jody. *Oh, that could have been us. I think I would die if anything happened to my Jody.'* She wondered about the wisdom of her decision to go on working for awhile. If she hadn't been so hard-headed, they'd be married right now facing the uncertain future together. That was a big trip for her.

Penny's delight in her job was reinforced on her next flight when she met her star passenger. Chimpanzee celebrity Mr. Muggs attracted a crowd at the Birmingham Airport. Dressed in a sailor suit, white hat with streamers, and black patent buckle shoes, he delighted Penny when, after climbing the steps to their Convair flight, he turned and threw kisses to the crowd. His trainer showed Penny two boarding passes and she helped them get situated near the center of the cabin. During her stewardess duties, she was amazed as Mr. Muggs acted like a person. The chimp even marked a big X on a page in her autograph book, a purchase she had quickly made after having Jimmy Stewart on board. When the flight landed in Atlanta, a newspaper reporter took her picture shaking hands goodbye with Mr. Muggs. When the print appeared, Penny was dismayed to see him more photogenic than she. "That cinches it! I won't ever get a darn monkey for a pet. Maybe a nice, ugly boa constrictor instead!"

One morning when Penny was alone in the apartment, the phone rang. It was crew scheduling asking her to take a football charter to California even though she was no longer on reserve. Crew scheduling said they would rearrange her regular rotation if she would take the charter. They were short on reserves and had chosen to call her since she wasn't scheduled out on a regular run for four more days.

"Sho nuff. I'll be glad to take the team to California. It will get me away from this awful Atlanta weather. When do we depart?

"Right now!"

"Appreciate the advance notice. I'm on my way, curlers and all. Rev up the engines!'

As she boarded the plane with the other stewardess, they started checking supplies and Penny was amazed to find no milk for the boys' breakfasts. She asked the caterer about it. He replied that they didn't need it, but she ordered fifty half-pints anyway, as a special order. She knew that great big football players drank a lot of milk. The flight was delayed while the caterer got the milk. The pilot demanded an explanation and after talking with Penny, he radioed the tower and had the delay put on record as stewardess holding, charging the delay to the stewardess department rather than to the pilot department of Southaire Corporation. Penny was confident there would be no repercussions when she explained to her supervisor and wrote it up on her flight record.

After they were in the air with fifty ball players and some coaches and sponsors, the girls served breakfast. They asked each passenger "Milk or coffee?"

Not one single person wanted milk. They wanted orange juice and coffee, but no milk. They said they had to drink it in the dormitory and were tired of it so did not want it on their special flights. Penny and her junior stewardess were getting exasperated with the burley boys. "Now look, gang, ya gotta drink milk. It's good for you. You need it to win the game!"

"No thanks, but how about some more orange juice" was the answer in all cases.

Penny gave an imitation of Al Jolson on bent knee to the group in the lounge seats . . . "Pppppllllllllllleeeeeeeaaaaas-sssseeee. Pppppllllllllleeeeeeeaaaaaassssssseeeeee drink milk. Soak your feet in it, wash your hair in it, but do something with milk, for goodness sake, fellows."

"Nope! Coffee! Coffee! Coffee! Yea, yea, yea, coffee! Coffee! Coffee!" The chant filled the cabin. Penny and the stewardess escaped into the buffet area and pulled their curtains. Penny looked disgusted. "What in the Sam Hill am I going to do with fifty cartons of milk between now and landing in California? I took a stew hold and delayed this flight for this darn milk. I can't pour it in the john because sanitation would report something wrong with the holding tanks if they were all white when we land. I can't pour it out an open window because we're pressurized. Think partner, think! What are we going to do with all this milk?"

"Not we Penny. Thee!"

"I can put some of it in my suitcase, but not fifty cartons. Have you got any room in your suitcase, just till we get to the hotel?"

"Nope! I'm packed solid."

"I wonder if one of the pilots would let me put my clothes in his flight bag."

"They probably don't have room. They keep those things stuffed with maps and updates on their procedures manuals. Besides, how you gonna explain why you want him to carry your clothes? They weren't too darn happy with a delay in the first place and they're trying to make it up now so we'll arrive as expected. You are aware there will be a crowd waiting to meet this charter, aren't you? And those crowds don't like to be kept waiting, especially for their football team's foes. They're anxious to get a look at these guys and size them up."

"Wonder if one of the players has got an extra suitcase?"

"Forget it Penny. Admit on your flight report that you made a mistake and chalk it up to experience."

"Never!"

While they were in the buffet staring at the milk cartons, one of the players came in through the curtains with a blanket wrapped around his body. "Stewardess, I spilled coffee on my pants and one of the fellows went to wash it off. Must have been cheap pants. The color ran all over my legs and left them blue. Would you like to see?"

The other stew exited quickly with a "No thanks!"

Penny stood open-mouthed. "Of course I don't want to see! I'll take your word for it. Why don't you just go back and sit down until your buddy brings your pants back to you."

"But miss, look! I burned my leg. Look!' He started to unwrap the blanket.

"Wait a minute. Wait! Let me get my medical kit and get some burn salve."

"My buddy also took my shorts to wash."

Penny exclaimed, "Hold it just a sec. Let me get you the salve and you put it on your leg. Don't unwrap the blanket any more, please."

"Ta dah!" He snatched off the blanket. His spotless trousers were rolled up to his knees. At her dismayed expression, he laughed in triumph.

After she finally conceded that he had played a good joke on her, he stayed in the buffet to talk a few minutes. "I'm Bobby Clinton, right end."

"Penny Perkins. Glad to know you, Bobby, I think."

"You girls are making this a real enjoyable flight. Are you coming to the game?"

"No. We're not staying with the charter this time. Two more stews working a rotation trip tomorrow to California will be bringing you back. We're changing with them and taking back their flight. We'll work their trip back tomorrow night and they will spend one night and then work your charter back on Sunday."

"I'd rather have you."

"Thank you."

"Too bad. I was gonna ask you to go out after the game."

"Well, that's the way it goes sometime. You better roll down your pants legs. They're gonna get awfully wrinkled."

"Yeah, guess I'd better. Guess I'd better get out of here and stop pestering you so you can get your work done." Glancing at the stack of red and white cartons, he pointed. "You really like milk, don't you?"

"Not really, but I sure do wish some of you guys did."

"Oh we like it fine. We were just teasing you girls. We know about the delay for this milk and what you went through for us. The caterer was grumbling about it to our coach. We'll drink the milk before we land. Here, I'll help you pass out the cartons now."

"Hey, Bobby, thanks!" She grabbed him in a big hug. "You just saved my hide."

Grinning, he said, "For this kind of reward, I'd save your life any time. But, it'll cost you a date some time."

"You're on."

When the players were deplaning in Los Angeles, Bobby leaned over and kissed Penny on the cheek. "See ya in Hot-lanta."

She winked at him but didn't offer her unlisted phone number.

On the return flight a gentleman in the forward section stopped her as she was gathering magazines to pass out. "May I have Modern Farming, please young lady?"

Taken with surprise, Penny blurted, "Why on earth do you want that one! Nobody ever reads it! I pass it every time I pass magazines and it's always the one I take back and put in the rack. It looks brand new even when it's outdated. I'm amazed that you've asked for it so you must tell me why!"

"I am the editor!"

"What can I say?"

"Do you have to say anything else at all?"

"Guess not."

"Then don't"

"Would you like . . ."

"Nothing! Absolutely nothing!"

"Yes, sir."

The flight made two stops enroute from Los Angeles to Atlanta. At the second stop, a nice looking guy gave the girls a big smile as he boarded. They automatically (as they were taught to do in stewardess training) glanced at his third finger, left hand. Sure enough, there was a wedding band. Later, as they were serving dinner he asked Penny for a date when they landed in Atlanta. She noticed that he had removed his ring.

Annoyed, she looked him straight in the eye. "Would you like for me to help you look for your wedding band before we land? Perhaps it just rolled under your seat." He turned red and quickly averted his gaze toward the setting sun. Even when he was getting off he kept his eyes straight ahead and didn't look at her. Neither did the modern farmer editor.

Jane and Penny had each swapped around trips with other stews. They found to their very pleasant surprise they were going to fly together.

"Well, I'll be darned, Jane. After all this time we get the chance to prove to Southaire we're the best team they've got."

They shared a cab to the airport, readied their clipboard forms, boarded the plane and executed the preparations necessary before the passengers arrived. Jane stood at the door to greet them and Penny started hanging coats and putting personal belongings in the overhead rack.

One grumpy passenger with a face like a Basset hound did not want to go to all the trouble to take his boarding pass ticket out of his pocket to show to Jane. "Just take my word for it, I have a ticket."

"I'm sorry, sir. I have to see your boarding pass. I have to check you in."

"I'm on the right plane. I've flown before. Just don't bother me. I have a ticket." He shoved past her bumping into

Penny who was in the aisle writing check cards for collected coats and wraps. He didn't even apologize. Penny looked at his retreating figure, and then raised her eyebrows at Jane who was peeping around the buffet curtain to see where the man was going.

When they were taxiing to the end of the runway, Penny was checking seat belts in the forward cabin while Jane was working the aft. When Penny got to the rude man, she said politely, "Please fasten your seat belt for takeoff, sir."

"It bothers me to fasten it. I'll be alright. Just leave me alone."

"Sir, you have to fasten it. The Civil Air Board prohibits our taking off with seat belts unfastened. You must fasten it for takeoff."

"Oh, hell! Alright" He loosely buckled it with a resounding snap and glared at her.

She smiled sweetly. "Thank you, sir. I do hope you have the most pleasant flight of your life today, sir."

Scurrying to jump into a seat as the DC-7 picked up speed down the runway, Penny buckled in next to Jane. "We have the original pickle king up in 7A."

"Glad he's in your section instead of mine."

"Want to swap sections?"

"Not on your tin-type, goose! He's all yours."

"Roommates are supposed to share. We'll share him.'

"Thanks."

His bell was the first to signal for a stewardess. Penny hurried forward. "Yes, sir?"

"When you bring my breakfast tray, put an ice cube in my coffee. Airline coffee is too strong."

"Perhaps you might prefer hot tea."

"That wasn't what I asked for, was it?"

"One ice cube coming up, sir."

"Bring your official airline guide. I want you to plan some connecting flights into Southampton and then have your pilot radio ahead for reservations."

"Well, uh, do you mind if we do that after we serve the meal? It's warm and ready and most people like their breakfast while it's hot."

"I want the reservations made right away. That is part of your duty. It will be a close changeover and I want confirmation by radio now."

"Oh yes, sir. I know it's my duty and I will be most happy to plan your continuation in just a few minutes, but it would be a bit more convenient after we serve the meal."

"Are you refusing to help me?"

"No, sir!" she replied through clenched teeth.

"Bring the book!"

In a whispered conference with Jane, it was agreed that Jane would start serving and Penny would help just as quickly as possible. In a few minutes, the complicated routes were recorded, a satisfactory set of advance reservations were requested and confirmation would be radioed back as soon as possible. Without a thank you, the man reminded Penny "Don't forget the ice cube in my coffee."

After the meal service was over and second coffees were offered, the trays were picked up and the buffet area cleared. The girls then went in the cabin to offer more personalized service to their passengers by cheerily visiting, offering pillows and magazines and spicing up the trip a bit for the ones receptive to conversation.

Grouch was not receptive. He didn't like the magazines Jane happened to be passing out. He thought the pillow had an odor and after trying four more, he decided they all had odors. Jane met his challenge and decided to make that man enjoy at least one thing on Southaire's line if she never did another good deed for her company. "Why don't you look out the window? There is some beautiful scenery and it is such a sparkling day. We're flying low enough for you to see rivers and farmland, and even an occasional lost little drifting blue cloud. Be happy. Look out the window and enjoy nature."

"I don't want to look out the window."

Without a thought of any consequences, Jane dropped her load of magazines, grabbed his head in exasperation and turned it toward the window. "I said, look out the window!"

Shocked at what she had done, she quickly turned his face toward her and was astonished to see that his eyes were tightly clenched closed in stubborn refusal to even respond to the strength of her emotion. She knew her job would be more secure if she kept quiet and vented her anger by kicking the battle scarred metal strip on the bottom of the buffet door, but she could not hold back.

"Mister, you can go to hell!"

Chapter 11—Put Him on a Bus

Winter, with its wet and cold, blanketed the South. Penny felt terrible as she prepared for what she felt would be her last flight before she succumbed to a cold. Luck seemed to have deserted her. She found out at crew sked (scheduling) that she was assigned to a milk run flight—a Convair that stopped at every town big enough to have an airport between Atlanta and Dallas. To make matters worse the name of the regularly scheduled pilot was crossed out and McLain Saranata written in.

"Oh boy, I've heard about him," she muttered aloud. "He's been flying since the Wright brothers and thinks he owns the airline. Just my luck that he's swapped with somebody and got on my flight. Jane says he's a terror. I'll try to avoid him as much as I can."

"Hey skirt, ya gonna stand there all day? If you're gonna fly on my air-o-plane with me youse better get moving." A deep voice boomed behind her. She turned and saw a dark, stocky man with grey salting his temples glaring at her from a hands-on-the hip position.

"I'm boarding now, Sir."

She dashed out the door and across the wet runway. "Oh boy, I wish I was home in bed."

She saw Mac again only briefly as he came aboard and the pre-takeoff preparations were made. Her cold was catching up with her as she tried to perform her duties with a forced heartiness.

One passenger, John Delano, was supposed to deplane in Shreveport, but he was asleep when they landed. Nearing the last leg of the long trip, fatigue made Penny careless about checking her seating chart and when she saw Mr. Delano sleeping blissfully, she hoped the onboarding passengers would not wake him. She wished she were napping in his place. When the agent came to pick up the seat count, the flight was one passenger over the number turned in by the ticket counter but because Penny was feeling so terrible, they both assumed she just couldn't count. The agent quickly returned with manifest and clearance for take off. About midway between Shreveport and Dallas, John Delano woke. Penny offered him a cup of coffee. "This will give you time to get your eyes open and wash your face before landing. You really must be tired. You slept right through the last stop."

"Is Shreveport the next one?"

"No sir. It was the last one, the one you snoozed right through."

He sat up straight and handed her back the cup of coffee. "You mean we've already been to Shreveport?"

"Yep. Just relax. You'll be in Dallas in no time."

"I don't want to go to Dallas.

"Then why did you get on a Dallas flight?"

"It was the only way I could get to Shreveport."

"Whoops!" Penny realized what had happened. She just didn't know what to do about it. She took a nervous sip of his coffee, then, still not thinking clearly, she gave it back to him. He also took a sip of it and looked at her.

"Well? Not we, Miss Perkins. You! You have a problem. I want to go to Shreveport. I bought a ticket aboard Southaire to go to Shreveport. I checked the weather for Shreveport before I left Atlanta. It is clear, so there was no chance of having to bypass Shreveport on this flight. I have plans in Shreveport. And you should have seen that I got off in Shreveport.

"Well . . . I guess I'd better go confer with my captain. He might have a suggestion."

The walk to the cockpit seemed like the legendary longest mile. He'll kill me! I'm dead! Confer with my captain, I said! I should have said 'get executed' by my captain.

She braced herself and opened the cockpit door. Both pilots were laughing at a joke Mac was telling. Penny burst right into a quick but concise explanation of the problem with Delano. Staring past Captain Saranata at a light on the instrument panel, she took complete blame for the mishap hoping that he wouldn't reprimand her.

"Ya innerrupted my story to tell me that?"

"Yes sir, Captain Saranata. I have to do something."

"Well, what are ya gonna do?"

"I, uh, thought you might have a suggestion about what I can do."

"Ya got any money?" Mac winked at the copilot.

"Some. Not a whole lot."

"Ya got enough to buy a ticket back to Shreveport for this guy?"

"I could write a check."

"How about bus fare. Got enough for that?"

"Oh I wouldn't put him on a bus, Captain Saranata. He'd never fly Southaire again if I did that."

"That's true. His letter to the company would really be something."

"Oh yes it would."

"Ya know, newspapers love to print little stories about airline bloopers. Make sure he doesn't start fussing too loud."

"Oh, I will. I'll tell him to keep it quiet."

"Naw, don't tell him that. Then he'll think he has something on Southaire and he'll sue us for a bundle."

The copilot was furiously biting his lip trying to keep from laughing. Penny was trying to pick up a clue, any way she could to appease Mr. John Delano. "Oh, that's right. What am I going to do? I just feel horrible about this happening."

He noticed her watering eyes. "Ya don't have to cry about it. It ain't that bad."

"I'm not crying. I have a cold."

"Then what da hell ya flying fer? That's the worst thing ya can do, fly with a cold. Ya not only take a chance of rupturing ya eardrums, ya give everybody else ya germs. Stupid broads! Now I'll probably catch ya cold and have to stay home and my Pauline don't want me hanging 'round the house."

"I'm sorry. It's not a bad cold and I'm just starting it. Anyway that's not the problem. What am I gonna do about Mr. Delano?"

"Aw go tell him Southaire will book him on the next flight to Shreveport or wherever he will go."

"They will?"

"Certainly. They do it all the time. You skirts don't got enough sense to keep up with your passengers and the company knows it. Now go buckle everyone in. We're approaching love field in Dallas."

Sitting beside John Delano during landing, Penny explained, "My captain suggested you go to Dallas with us, and then we will return you to Shreveport on the next flight. While you are in Dallas, we will treat you to anything you want to eat or drink. And there will be no charge for your return trip to Shreveport.'

"No charge to return me to Shreveport, my original destination, the place I bought a ticket for."

"I must have said that wrong." Penny eyed his coffee. "If you don't want that, Mr. Delano . . ."

"I don't need anything to wake me up now. Here you finish drinking it. You need to wake up more than I do. How soon can I get another flight?"

"I'll get the airline guide as soon as we land. Don't worry! We'll get you back as soon as possible. I just feel dreadful that this happened." Tears rimmed her eyes.

He patted her hand. "Don't worry, honey. I have a sister in Dallas. I'll call her. Might even spend the night and go to Shreveport in the morning. Mistakes happen. Please don't cry. I'm not that upset and I'll fly Southaire again.

Penny deadheaded home to Atlanta. She was too sick to work her scheduled return portion. She was out of work for ten days and when she finally was able to resume flying, it was with anticipation.

After that first day back on the job, Penny burst into the apartment that night. "Jane, Jane, I had my favorite movie

star today on 409 coming back from New Orleans. At least I
think it was him."

Jane came into the room with a towel wrapped around her
fresh-washed hair. "Slow down, goose, and make sense, will
you?"

"I had Tab Hunter on my flight. Oh I adore him. Those
blonde, square-jawed guys just get to me. I think it was him.
I'm positive it was Tab Hunter."

"You telling me or asking me, Penny?"

She dropped her shoulder purse onto the couch. "Well, I
think it was Tab Hunter. He was traveling under an assumed
passenger name and he never would admit it was him. We
kept on after him to tell us the truth but he kept saying we
had him confused with someone else. But, Jane, I know it
was the real Tab Hunter."

"How come he wouldn't admit it?" She began rubbing her
wet hair briskly.

"He just wouldn't admit it. I think he was just teasing us
but he swore up and down he was not Tab Hunter. I swear up
and down it was. Anyway, he wouldn't give me his autograph
so I'm tempted to write it in myself in my autograph book."

"Dumb, dumb. The whole idea of the book is to get their
signatures in your book, not to fill it up yourself with names."
She attempted to run her fingers through her sticky wet hair.
"One of these days I'm gonna splurge on a wig if I never buy
another thing."

A few days later a 12 x 16 autographed glossy of the smiling Tab Hunter arrived at Southaire's Chief Stewardess office for Penny Perkins. It was signed, *To my favorite stew
from your mystery guy.* Penny wasted no time in showing the
picture to everyone.

The picture was prominently displayed in the apartment
when Jody arrived for a visit.

"Penny, how do you know Tab Hunter? You been dating
him?"

"No, honey. He was just a passenger on one of my flights.
It's his idea of a joke," she explained, then patted his hand.

"Make yourself comfy and tell me the old hometown gossip while I put the final touches on our dinner. I've planned a real romantic meal for us. It's hard to realize you're finally here for a visit. I've wanted you to come and see our bachelor girl apartment. I've especially wanted to see you. I'm really thrilled you're here, Jody." She put the brown and serve rolls in the oven.

He stood in the kitchenette archway. "I've missed you so much, Penny, I could hardly stand it. It's like a dream come true having you this close, having you cook my dinner. Say, do you girls have a hi-fi?"

"Sure. Right over there in the corner." She gestured with a pot holder. He went over and leafed through their collection of records, finally choosing an instrumental. He returned to watch her in the kitchen as the soft strains of music filled the tiny apartment.

Penny cocked her head. "Oooohhhhhh, that's pretty. That must be Jane's newest record. I didn't know we had that. Romantic music matches my mood."

"Can you get the lid off these olives?" She thrust the jar at Jody. "You know olives are a passion food." He pulled her toward him.

She ducked out of his arms. "Watch it, Jody, or I'll never get this meal on the table. Honey, would you get the champagne from the ice box and open it? My roomy, Narda, swiped it from a champagne charter just for us to have tonight."

"Ah, I like Narda already without ever having met her. Shall I pour it? Where are you gonna sit?"

"Why? Are you going to pour more champagne in my glass and get me pie-eyed before dinner?"

"Now Penny, honey, you know I wouldn't entertain a notion like that."

While she was involved with whipping cream with a new portable electric mixer, Jody took advantage of the noise and Penny's preoccupation to slip a small blue velvet box from his pocket. Glancing once more at her, he opened the box and removed a platinum band adorned with a single diamond. He dropped it in her champagne glass where it sank and lay camouflaged by the storm of rising bubbles.

She finished putting the meal on the table, beamed with pride, then grabbed a match and handed it to Jody. "Here sweetheart, you light the candles while I turn out the lights all over the apartment."

"Things are getting better all the time." He sneaked a quick glance at her champagne glass and was reassured to see the bubbles still rising. He held out her chair for her and they sat down to the carefully prepared meal.

He lifted his glass. "Darling, I want to propose a toast. It isn't original but I'm saying it for the first time. To foreverness with you."

They tinkled glasses. He half drained his. She took a sip, and then put her glass down. "What's the matter, Penny? Don't you like champagne?"

"Oh sure, but let's eat. Here, have some French cut beans."

He nervously sipped champagne between bites trying to get her to follow suit. She seemed oblivious to her champagne, as well as her engagement ring at the bottom of the glass. She was occupied with excited chatter and plying Jody with her home-cooked food.

"What happened to your rancher's appetite? Here, have some more roast beef. There's plenty."

He picket up the champagne bottle and refilled his glass looking expectantly at her glass. "Honey, drink your champagne before it gets warm."

"What is wrong with you, Jody? I've never seen you so jumpy. Is something bothering you? You've hardly touched this meal. If you need to be excused, it's just right there in the hall."

He slammed his fist on the table. "Dammit, Penny, drink your champagne!"

Stunned, she picked up her glass and indignantly, retorted, "Well, all right!" Taking a big swallow, she felt the ring touch her lips. She held her glass up to the candlelight and seeing the object within her face puckered. "Oh Jody, my ring! I love it! I love you! I'm gonna cry!" She jumped up to hug him.

After their embrace, he carefully removed her ring, wiped it with a napkin and slipped it on her awaiting finger. "I love you with all my heart, Penny. I want you to be my wife. Would you like to set a date?"

"Oh, Jody. It's a beautiful ring and I love you too. I've loved you a long time. Thank you for my ring. I'll wear it with pride."

"A date, Penny? The wedding day? When?" They drifted toward the sofa.

"Oh Jody, I don't know. Some time in June. I'd like to be a June bride and of course we'll have a church wedding. I'll want my roommates here as bridesmaids and Pat, my roommate in college, as my maid of honor. Yeah, sweetheart, a June wedding."

"Sounds good. Pick a magic number and get on with it." He squared her toward him on the sofa. "Penny, are you sure? What about flying?"

She looked into his hazel eyes and replied in a soft, serious voice. "Yes, Jody, I'm sure. I've loved being a stew and I wouldn't trade this past year for anything, but the travel itch is just about out of my system and I want to be married to you and live the rest of our lives in Texas on the ranch with kids and cattle and everything running around us." She paused. "One thing I haven't done is go to Europe. Would it bother you if, before I resign from Southaire, if I . . .?"

He squeezed her shoulders gently. "Honey, have your big trip. Go ahead, you deserve it. Now that I know you're coming home to me, I don't mind if you go all the way around the world.'

As they eased onto the sofa, Jody began nibbling at Penny's earlobe. She nestled blissfully against him, her breath warm on his neck. "Jody, I do love you and I'm proud of my ring. It's so pretty and so big. I'm all excited about us getting married. Are you sure you don't mind me going to Europe first? I've alwayss wanted to go to Europe and this may be my only chance."

"Well, thanks, Penny! You don't think I'll be able to take you to Europe some day?"

"Oh honey, I didn't mean that. I meant while I can still get interline passes and discounts and it's just something I want to do before I quit being a stewardess. Do you want to argue?" She pushed back from his embrace to glare at him.

He pulled her closer. "No I just want to make love to you."

Her words were muffled against his shirt front. "Well, you can't do that just yet. We've waited through four years of college. And a year of my fling and we can wait a little bit longer." She sighed as if the matter was settled.

His hand dropped down beyond the small of her back. "Maybe you can wait but I can't. Honey, we're engaged now. It will be alright!"

She pushed away to stare at him. "Jody Stinsen, you know we're gonna be married in the church and I'm gonna wear white and we're gonna take our vows before God and everybody and we're not gonna do it under false pretenses and that's that." She wagged a finger in his face. "Jody, I want to tell you something. I want you just as much as you want me, but I was brought up in a church-going family and it's a part of me. We'll just have to tough it out until after our wedding. I feel real strong about being married in my church and that's just something you're gonna have to share with me."

He arose. "Okay, okay Penny, I get the message. But boy, you'd better look out when we get married." He reached down and pulled her to her feet.

She kissed him quickly. "No, you'd better look out when we get married."

His eyes widened. "Promise?"

She twitched her hips. "Do I ever!"

On Penny's next night coach flight, five passengers in the lounge area had a bottle. They mixed their own drinks and weren't bothering the other passengers. Penny and her junior stewardess got the cabin settled down and passed magazines to the few insomniacs who couldn't slumber. Occasionally they took ice and water to the partying people in the lounge. It was a fairly routine flight. Penny sat down about mid-cabin to visit with an elderly lady traveling to be with her only son who was dying of cancer. "He is such a brilliant young man, a research chemist and as fate would have it, he was conducting experiments on cancer cells when he found out about his brain tumor."

Penny nodded. "Things like this always make us wonder why some people, really useful people, have such a limited time on Earth."

The lady turned to her. "Do you ever get frightened? Are you ever afraid of a crash?"

Penny looked at her with unblinking honesty. "No ma'am, I'm really not. They ask us that in stewardess training. I guess I have pretty much the same thoughts along those lines as the majority of stews. I feel when my time comes it will happen no matter where I may be. And the joke, yeah, but what if it's the pilot's time, doesn't upset me. If it's not my time to go, then I'll be a survivor even if it's both pilots' time. Or if I'm not a survivor, I do believe in the hereafter. I'm not fearful of death. I'm a Christian. Sometimes not a very good one, I must admit, but I do honestly believe when I die that I'll go to heaven and if I should be killed in a plane crash, then I'll already have on my wings. But, I'm not afraid of a crash. And Southaire really does have an excellent safety record. Can I get you some hot tea or anything? I need to go check on my passengers again."

"No thanks, my dear."

She heard the giggling coming from the lounge about the time she got up from her seat. The overhead light was out and the sprinkling of night lights barely illuminated the rear of the DC-7 twilight coach.

As she made her way rearward, a figure stood up. It was a man, a naked man. Penny halted in surprise, and then edged forward. Everyone in the lounge area was naked, two women and three men. They were involved in a card game and as Penny arrived on the scene, one lady was pulling off her wedding band, the last vestige of covering she had on her body. "That's it! I lose! I never was any good at poker."

Penny flipped on the overhead light, and then quickly switched it off. They all looked at her with disinterest.

She grabbed a couple of blankets from the overhead rack and handed them to the man standing. "Please wrap yourself in this and help your friends cover themselves. And please sit down."

"Uh uh, little lady. I don't wanna sit. I been sittin' all day. Wanna stand and play cards with my friends?"

"The card game is over. We will be landing in Washington in just a few minutes. I suggest you try to get dressed before the overhead lights are turned on."

"Would you get me some more ice, pretty little lady?" He attempted to engulf her in a one-armed hug.

Penny side stepped him and threw the blankets at the seated passengers. Keeping her eyes directly on his face, she commanded, "Sit down and cover yourself immediately. Fasten your seat belt and stay put until we land. All the rest of you fasten your seat belts. Don't try to get up now and get dressed. It is too late. We are already on the approach down to Washington. You'll have to wait till after we land to get dressed."

The standing man sauntered over and slouched down into his seat. "You're a picky thing. I'm going to report you. Where's your sense of adventure?" Someone handed him a part of the blanket. He threw it aside.

Penny quickly got a couple more blankets and handed them around in the lounge area. Then she went to the public announcement mike for her approach speech before landing. She was upset. Even though it was against the rules, she remained in the buffet area standing and holding on while the plane touched down on the runway. As soon as the crew had reversed props (propellers) and the thrust of the plane had settled down into a roll along the runway toward the terminal, Penny rang the cockpit. "I have five drunk, naked people in the lounge. One man is belligerent and will probably give us a hard time. I know we will need some help. Will you notify airport security to meet this flight? Thanks. Oh shut up! I didn't look!"

Penny stood guard near the lounge area, while the junior stewardess bid the passengers farewell at the doorway. As soon as the passengers were off, two uniformed guards came aboard and went into the lounge area. The participants were passing another bottle and had not bothered to put on their clothes. The flight crew and the junior stewardess also came to the lounge area. The inebriated card players, faced with that many uniforms, finally relented and began slowly dressing themselves in a half way. The standing man was the only hold-out and he shouted. "I know my rights. You can't make me do anything I don't want to do!" He was carried bodily from the plane draped in a blanket, hollering the whole time. His cohorts followed meekly, trailing various pieces of clothing behind them.

Inside the terminal, Penny encountered the older lady and wished her extra strength when she visited her son at the hospital.

The lady smiled. "I saw and heard what happened in the rear of our plane. If I have just half your stamina, my dear, I'll be just fine." She patted Penny's arm and walked away.

Penny's next flight was a non-stop to Miami departing ATL at 2100. Just before the agent brought the clearance, a middle aged man and woman came rushing aboard carrying two large white boxes from a bakery. "Our niece just got married and they are taking this flight for their honeymoon. They are on their way through the terminal now. After you get airborne, will you please cut these cakes and give everyone on board a piece and tell them it is to help celebrate the wedding of Alicia Norton, uh Petrionilli now. His name is Phil. Anyway, this is a surprise for them so perhaps even your passengers might shout surprise or something when you pass out this wedding cake. We gotta run. Thank you.

Thank you very much." With a wave, they rushed to a doorway further away than the one their niece was just emerging from trailed by a group of well-wishers tossing rice.

In a few minutes the flight was winging south toward Miami. After settling their passengers, Penny and the other stew went to each seat and whispered about the newlyweds on board and solicited their help in shouting congratulations as soon as the stews gave the signal and started passing cake.

The Petrionillis were seated midway the cabin. Putting one of the cakes on a serving tray, Penny and her helper took it to show the young couple. As they reached the newlyweds seat, the other stew gave a signal and everyone on board yelled, "Surprise! Congratulations!" as Penny showed them the wedding cake. Then a few started singing "Here comes the bride, big, fat and wide, doggone her hide, here comes the bride!"

With embarrassed looks at each other, the couple started laughing, then stood up and bowed to the crowd, both fore and aft, then waved to a few well-wishers who were waving. Alicia threw a few kisses and Phil looked bright-eyed and handsome.

While the stewardesses were serving cake, turbulence was encountered. As the last pieces of cake were being given out, the Fasten Seat Belts sign flashed on. Again the plane bounced and the girls hurried to check seat belts, and then buckled themselves in. The plane continued to bob about. A pilot's voice crackled over the system. "Ladies and gentlemen, we are going to land in Jacksonville for a few minutes due to extremely bad weather ahead. The front is passing and we should be able to continue into Miami in a short time. Please remain seated until we are on the ground. Do not leave the plane in Jacksonville. We will only be there for a few minutes or until the weather front passes this area. Please be assured that Southaire is doing this for your safety and we regret any inconvenience in flight delay."

After they had been on the ground in Jacksonville an hour, the passengers were allowed to deplane and go inside the terminal. In four hours their flight departure was announced and the plane took off for Miami.

Fog had settled over Miami. The flight was put into a holding pattern and began circling the area. At 3:30 a. m. they had been circling for an hour. They continued circling as long as possible, then landed at Ft. Lauderdale for refueling. Snack bar facilities were made available for the famished passengers who eagerly deplaned for refreshments. After eating and walking about to relieve stiff muscles, they were anxious to go on, but Miami was still socked in with ground fog. Four hours later they were airborne again.

After circling for two more hours, they finally landed in Miami at noon on Saturday. The honeymooning couple, along with everyone else on board, was exhausted. As Phil and Alicia Petrionilli left the plane for what was left of their weekend honeymoon in Miami, Phil quipped. "You all must join us on our next honeymoon, too. We would be lonesome without you!"

Penny retorted, "Well, you know how it is. If you have time to spare, go by air!"

When Penny returned to her apartment at midnight, she was one tired fly girl. Jane was up watching television. Penny shook her head. "Don't ask! Let's just plan our vacation to get us as far away from the Southaire Corporation as possible."

"Europe?"

"Where else?"

Chapter 12—Across the Big Pond

Groggy from time changes, a memorable bon voyage party given by their roommates, and an unaccustomed champagne breakfast, Jane and Penny dozed intermittently the entire flight from New York.

Rubbing her eyes, Penny tried to focus. "Where are we?" She shook Jane who was snoozing beside her. "Jane, sit up. Wake up. We've arrived."

"Ummmm . . . where?"

"I don't know. Where were we supposed to land first?

" Ummmm . . . huh?"

"Jane! Wake up!" Penny jabbed her with a sharp left elbow jab. "C'mon. Everybody's getting off the plane. We've got to get our stuff."

"Comin', comin'. I'm coming! Where are my shoes?" Jane tried to bend forward to look under her seat. "Ouch! Lightening just struck my head."

"Yeah! White lightening! C'mon." She started sing-songing. "We're in Europe. We're on vacation. We're lovely. We use Ponds!"

"Penny! Please don't entertain me right now! Okay?"

"Grrrr to you too, roommate!"

As they neared the green trimmed white building, a large sign above the door way greeted them- Welcome to Shannon, Ireland. They went into the cool, tidy restaurant and were waited upon by a trim girl in a light green uniform. After a big breakfast, they began to gather their thoughts.

Wandering into the souvenir shop, Penny purchased Jody a tan cashmere sweater and a white one for herself. "Nothing like trousseau shopping in Ireland!"

Jane rallied. "Now that we're here and I've decided I'll live, let's make the most of our stopover and see some sights."

They went into the town of Shannon. On the short journey they realized why Ireland is called The Emerald Isle. The overwhelming impression was of cool, damp, living green-ness. Wide, verdant meadows were dotted with snowy sheep. Immaculate whitewashed cottages nestled amidst well-kept gardens. The whole world seemed freshly scrubbed and wide awake.

They were scheduled out on an evening flight, so they returned after a short excursion to the airport with arms full of souvenirs and feeling much better after having caught some of the infectious, live Irish spirit.

They landed in Brussels, Belgium, about 9:00 p.m. and went into the restaurant to treat themselves to a big steak dinner, having missed lunch. The waiter came to take their order. He didn't understand English and they knew no foreign language, so they used sign language to order what was not on the menu. He bowed and grinned, then hurried to the kitchen. He brought salad, potatoes, wine and coffee. In a few minutes he returned with their steaks. The meat was nearly raw. Jane took one look. "I can't eat this. It has to be well done for me."

"Me too. This looks like it hasn't even been cooked."

They beckoned the waiter and tried to tell him what was wrong. He didn't understand but took their steaks back to the kitchen. In a few minutes he returned with another steak for each, still very rare. They shook their heads and handed the plates back to him. Understanding dawned on his face. He made another trip rearward. He reappeared with the chef behind, bowing and grinning, with larger but still underdone steaks. They didn't want larger pieces of meat but they didn't know what to do. The chef was grinning and waiting for them to start eating. With sad shakes of their heads and shrugs of shoulders, they moved the steaks aside and started eating the potatoes, trying vainly to return to smiles of satisfaction.

The chef pointed to the steaks. They gave him a pitiful look. Suddenly he stomped him feet, his face got red and he began making loud remarks and throwing his hands in the air.

The manager came over and they all began to shout at him, Penny, Jane, the waiter and the chef. He understood a little bit of English, so amid the confusion, he explained to the chef what they had wanted. Haltingly, he explained that it was an insult to a Cordon Bleu chef to refuse food that he personally delivered to a table. He was presenting a work of art.

After all was calmed, they ate a few bites, the paid their bill, and as they left, they could feel the cold, hard stares of the waiter, chef and manager, as well as those of the other customers. They felt like the center cog in spokes for an international incident.

Leaving Brussels, they headed for Paris. On the flight into France, Jane and Penny discussed Paris and what they thought it would be like.

"If I'm not mistaken, they don't have television yet anywhere in Europe, Jane. Of course we aren't going to Paris to watch television, but it isn't here anyway."

"Are you sure? I thought they did."

"Nope, not yet. They're a few years behind us in progress."

"Attention, please. We are landing at Earl Field. Please fasten your seat belts."

As they were getting off the plane, Penny squeezed Jane's hand and whispered. "Golly, I'm so thrilled. Imagine me in Paris. It's a long way from Texas. Of course there is a Paris, Texas and I've been there, but it's nothing like this."

"Uh huh!"

They rode a bus from the airport to a terminal in the city. From there, they took a taxi to L'Hotel de la Rue de Bourgogne. Behind the small grillwork, a heavy, elderly woman sporting a mustache greeted them.

"Bonjour, Mademoiselles."

With as little motion and expression as possible, the concierge checked their passports, registered them, handed them a key and pointed the way to their room.

They rode a rickety, open cage type elevator to the third floor, found their room and unlocked the door. Entering through a small room containing a desk, chairs and a coat rack, they found a large bedroom with French doors opening onto a balcony overlooking the center square of the hotel. Delighted, they discovered a small floral garden with a fountain just below their window. Penny opened her eyes wide. "Reckon we got the right room? This seems awfully plush for an airline discount room."

From the bedroom they wandered into the huge bath and here the girls saw, for the first time, a bidet. "Wonder what that thing is next to the commode, eh, Penny?"

"Gosh, I don't know. Guess it is for the maid to wash her mop. See, it has two faucets on the back of it."

"Maybe it's a foot bath. The French people walk a lot and perhaps they soak their feet when the day is over." Jane walked around the bathroom, but her eyes were mostly on the little thing that resembled both a commode and a wash basin.

"Dubs on a bath first. I feel so dirty." Penny shouted from the bedroom. "But I'll hurry. I want to see something before bedtime."

"My dear Penny, in Paris, there is no such thing as bedtime."

But the warm bath did them in and they were asleep before the hour was over.

The next morning the two of them, dressed alike in floral skirts, white blouses, and flat shoes and toting their cameras, walked down the streets of Paris looking in store windows. They passed a jewelry shop, went inside and purchased a ring apiece for themselves depicting Paris, some perfume for their mothers, and bracelets for roommates Narda and Brenda. They continued to window shop as they strolled down the street. They happened to look in the window of a furniture shop and inside were a display of television sets. Not realizing what they had seen, they kept on walking. About a half block away Jane stopped abruptly, glared at Penny for a second and walked swiftly back to the furniture shop. Penny turned to catch up with her friend. Pointing at the window, Jane exclaimed. "No TV in Paris, eh?"

In one of the infrequent dull moments they decided to call a friend of a friend that they had been told to look up. They went into the first store they saw and asked for the phone. In his best French-English sign language, the clerk explained that there was no phone in the store. He tried to explain about the public telephone building, and with the help of others in the store, they were able to understand they had to go to a special building to use the telephone.

They purchased a French-English dictionary and were able to find the public telephone building. Going inside, they saw a counter at one end of a large room with several men working at what looked like keyboards. In the same room, lining one side, several booths were set up with phones in them. There were also benches as in a train or bus station for waiting. In a smaller room, through an arch, there were more telephones. Penny walked into one of the booths, dropped a coin in the slot and asked for information. One of the men from the counter walked up to the booth and announced that he was information. Penny gave him the name of the person she wanted to contact.

The friend of a friend worked in a government building, so the call had to go through the French state department. They had to leave a message, and then wait for him to return their call. The whole procedure, with language barriers, took about two hours. By the time they got to talk to the man by the name of Jourdan, the vacationing stews were almost too weary to know what to say. Penny introduced herself, mentioned the mutual friend, told him where they were staying and before she could continue, he had government business that interrupted their call. After a short time of picture taking and walking, the two retired early to pamper their aching feet in the foot bath in their bathroom.

Jourdan's call woke them the next morning about 10:00 a.m. Jourdan asked if they would like to attend an automobile show and he promised to entertain them to make up for his abruptness on the phone the day before.

Delighted, they agreed to meet him at noon under the Eiffel Tower. They dressed in their best suits, hats and high heels. When they went downstairs for breakfast, the diner was closed, and there wasn't even a stale croissant available. They stuck a piece of gum each in their mouths and went merrily on their way to the famous Paris landmark for their rendezvous with Jourdan. Penny and Jane had only a few minutes to stare at the towering metal structure before they saw a man waving at them from the street.

They hurried to join the man walking toward them. He had a big grin on his deeply sun-tanned handsome face and appeared to be in his early thirties. When he smiled, deep dimples appeared in his cheeks, making him appear much more youthful.

He greeted the girls with outstretched hands, taking a hand of each in his two hands. "Don't tell me, let me guess. You with red hair, you are Jane? No? Oh, so sorry, my guess is wrong. Please forgive my mistake, also my English, which is, how you say, lousy? No?"

They laughed, linked their arms in his and walked to his car. "We go first to a cocktail party, oh, only a small one, for, how you say, V.I.P. people, then to ze automobile show. I zink you will enjoy eet. Eet eezs ze finest in all Paree. Ze cocktail party I have to be there because, how you say, eet eezs my duty."

Penny and Jane kept giving each other excited glances. They were enjoying his accent and were anticipating adventure.

As they walked in the door of the luxurious suite next to the showroom, they were handed a glass of champagne. Jourdan tried to introduce them to some of the other guests, but they were all talking French, and after a minute or two of trying, he shrugged his shoulders, excused himself and joined a group of men.

"Boy, this is good. Jane, old buddy, Jody and I are just gonna have to lay us in a supply of this brand out on the

ranch 'cause after this European vacation, I ain't gonna settle for bourbon and branch water."

Penny grinned at her friend who hadn't taken her eyes off
Jourdan since they met him. "Quite a guy, isn't he?"

As if caught at something, Jane quickly averted her look
back to Penny. "He's fascinating. I'm having a good time.
This champagne is great. Here comes the waiter with more.
Shall we?"

"Why not, we're on vacation. Ummm, the bubbles tickle.
I think we should have, how you say, eaten more for breakfast than a stick of gum."

They giggled. Finishing their third glass, they were beginning to need something to lean on when Jourdan appeared.

"Shall ve go now, my charming young ladies? The show
is underway and I want you to see some of our fine auto-
mobiles." He took them by their hands and led them from
the room. When they got outside, they realized they still had
their champagne glasses in their hands. Jourdan took the
glasses and put them gently on the floor. Jane, making an
attempt to grab hers for one last swallow, dropped her purse.
Penny got tickled and burst out laughing. Jourdan threw up
his hands and with "Bon Dieu", and then got down on the
floor with Jane to help gather all the things that had fallen
from her purse.

"How you American girls get so many things in one little space is amazing. Now do you have everyzing? Shall ve
go?"

The threesome entered an area three times as large as
Grand Central Station in New York. The room was filled with
every kind of automobile made in Europe. There were cars
every size from a three wheeled card table to a six wheeled
garage.

"Jane, look! Aren't those little ones adorable? I wish we
could afford to buy one, drive it all over Europe, then sell it
when we get ready to go back home. I would love to have
one of those little ones, red, maybe."

"Be practical, silly!"

They walked around the floor looking at the cars and asking Jourdan to translate the prices. Penny looked at the cars with a dreamy expression. "Gee, they're cheap. These cars sell for at least $500.00 more when they're shipped to America, Jourdan."

"Do you ladies like ze show?"

"It is wonderful!"

"We're enjoying it very much, Jourdan. Thank you."

"Now ve get something to eat. I will get my car and pick you up at the front entrance, right over there. Think you will be, how you say, ho-kay, until I return?"

They waved to him and walked to the front entrance slowly, looking at the people that milled about them. They waited just a few minutes before he drove up in his blue Citroen. "Ve go to sidewalk extraordinaire for coq au vin."

When they had finished the delicious meal, Jourdan ordered three small glasses of a dark brown liquid that turned a yellowish color when he added water to it.

"Drink and see how you like."

Penny was surprised to find it tasted just like licorice candy. "This is ze way to end a meal", Jourdan laughed. "Now suppose I take you to your hotel and pick you up later to, how you say, hit the night spots."

In their hotel room, Penny walked to the desk and sat down. "He is such a charming person. Ya know, Jane, Jourdan reminds me of all the movie stars who talk with a French accent. I'm gonna get Jody to take a French course with me after we get married so we'll be able to talk romantic to each other."

"Goose, how you and Jody speak to each other isn't the secret to romance. It's what you say that counts." She flopped on the bed. "Are you going to take a nap?"

"I think I will as soon as I write Jody. Whew, Jane, I can't keep up with the French in drinking. That was an odd after-dinner drink we had at that little sidewalk cafe. Ya know, I'm glad there are always two of us with Jourdan. He's quite worldly."

When Jourdan returned to escort them, Penny and Jane were dressed in their most fetching evening gowns. Jane was in a blue net, off the shoulder, and Penny wore a white strapless sheath that emphasized her curvaceous figure.

"Ze night is yours, Mesdemoiselles, tell me of your interest."

Simultaneously they answered, "Bohemian Left Bank."

"You both look merveilleux."

Presently they arrived at a nightclub called `Les Caves' and had to walk down a long, twisting staircase. Once inside, the girls got a look at what they had heard about the 'real' Paris.

The men were dressed in stripped tee-shirts with berets on their heads, and the women wiggled in tight, form fitting skirts slit up to the thigh of their leg. As they sat at a table, the band began to play a fast dance number and the Apache dancers moved about the floor in a rapid pace. The men began to sling the women over their shoulders as the music got faster and faster.

"Would either of you care to dance?" Jourdan offered.

"No, thanks. I'm afraid our dancing to rock and roll would seem mild compared to this."

"We'd rather just watch."

Jourdan ordered a bottle of anisette, the licorice tasting liqueur, and poured three drinks at their table. When the music changed to a slow number, he asked Jane to dance. When they were on the floor, he held her breathtakingly close.

When they returned to the table, Jane asked. "Have you never married, Jourdan?"

"Oh Cherie, I am married and have five children. I have been married, how you say, all my life. Suzette is a vonderful woman but is past her youth now, so she stays home most of the time. I invited her to join us tonight, but she declined and told me to have a good time. So tonight, I am not married. Tomorrow, yes! Tonight, no!"

Penny and Jane exchanged wide-eyed looks.

Penny exclaimed as she flashed her engagement ring. "I know I wouldn't be so liberal with my Jody."

"That is an American idea. Here the women are different. Their only thought is to make the man happy. She knows I am happy when I am out entertaining. I have to do a lot of entertaining in my job, but she always remains home. She makes me very happy when I am at home. Je l'aime très beaucoup."

They finished the bottle and when Jourdan offered to order another, they declined and asked him to show them more Paris nightlife.

After a few more clubs and a late, late dinner, they pled fatigue, and after bidding Jourdan goodnight in the wee hours of dawn, as they passed through the door of their hotel, they turned to each other with simultaneous exclamations. "He's married!"

"Jourdan is a married man. Five kids!"

"We've been out with a married man! What would they say in Atlanta?"

"I know what they would say in Texas!" Penny replied.

"Do you think we should still go with him to the Lido tomorrow night?"

"Gosh, Jane, I don't know. We can't go by ourselves. We have to have an escort, and we were with him a long time tonight."

"Yeah, but I feel funny knowing he's married. I felt funny the rest of the evening after he told us and I was embarrassed to sit next to him in the car."

"I know just what you mean. I wanted to talk to you about him, but we were moving so fast and furious all evening I never got the chance."

Throughout bedtime preparations, they discussed Jourdan. Jane finally said, "Well, back home we wouldn't go out again knowing what we know, but this is gay Paree!"

Penny replied with a mischievous leer. "Yeah, when in Paris, do as the Parisians."

Jane got up the next day at noon and woke Penny. Ravenous, they dressed quickly and went in search of food, knowing it was again too late for a hotel breakfast. They decided to go to the American Embassy because friends had told them they could get good old American hot dogs and hamburgers. They decided to walk and absorb more of the Parisian sights and smells.

Jane wore a flowery print dress with a matching cardigan thrown over her shoulders and Penny was dressed in a crinoline skirt with a matching blouse. As they entered the embassy, two young men strode out with signs on their backs that read 'From Texas'. They paused as the girls passed. Penny yelled "Hey! I'm from Texas."

Happy to meet other Americans, they asked if they might join them inside.

"Of course. We would love to talk to someone from home."

Penny and Jane were bubbling with excitement and quickly gave the waitress their orders. And then Penny said, "Okay, let's talk some Texas talk!"

The young men, both about eighteen, were bumming their way across Europe on a motorcycle and had already been there five months. They entertained with stories about sleeping in the open, eating with European country families and meeting interesting foreigners, both in the cities and in the countryside. They only had a few dollars left, but were planning to sell their motorcycle in another month to pay for their return voyage home. They explained that their only source of income was from a small newspaper chain in Texas for which they were writing articles about their travels and experiences. They received a money order each month in care of the American Express office in whatever European city they so designated.

Jane asked "What do you miss most since you are on such a limited funds tour?"

"We miss a bath with hot water . . . and haircuts. These are real luxuries to us. We take our baths in creeks and have had to let our hair get shaggy, as you can plainly see. Neither of us can cut hair."

Jane and Penny exchanged glances. After a whispered conference Penny spoke. "We've taken a vote and it is with pleasure that we offer you, free of charge, the use of our hotel bathroom and all the hot water you need."

"You're kidding?" they asked almost together.

"No, we mean it. You're welcome to use our room to clean up in if you make sure to mention our names in your next article for the papers."

The concierge gave them a knowing look as Penny and Jane led the two young men into the elevator and up to their room. Penny whispered to Jane, "She probably thinks the worst, after us coming in so late and being out with a married man, now 2 guys, but I really couldn't care less. It will give her something to ponder while she sits there, especially when the guys come down in different clothes."

"Doesn't bother me a bit either . . . much?" She grimaced.

They sat in their small room while Jason went in the bathroom. They could hear him singing and splashing as he remained in the bath for nearly an hour. When he joined them, he was freshly shaven and had on clean shirt and pants which were badly in need of ironing. He looked respectable again, except that his hair was so long that it curled about his neck down past his shirt collar. The other fellow, named Dave went into the bathroom as Jason talked with them. Penny brightened, excused herself and opened her suitcase. In a minute, she turned holding a little manicure kit in her hand.

"I've cut hair, women's hair before, so if you're willing, I'll give you a trim."

"Well now, ma'am, I don't know about that. Guess I'll give it a try though. I'll get a towel from the bathroom and you can cut away."

When she had finished, Penny and Jane stood back to view the work of art. Work of art it wasn't. It was a butch cut with his scalp showing through numerous gaps. "That's about the best I can do with these little scissors."

He let out a yelp when he crossed to the mirror. Dave appeared in the doorway pulling on his jeans. "Hey, what's all the shouting?" When he saw his friend, he shook his head. "Thanks, but no thanks. I'll pass on the haircut, but appreciate the bath, feel like I can go another six months now."

"Well, if you won't let me cut your hair, you'll have to leave. I'm teasing, but we do have to get ready for dinner, so we're gonna have to chase you away soon."

"Penny and Jane, we want to thank you. This is one of the nicest things that have happened to us on our trip. Can we take you to lunch sometime or something?" Dave offered.

Jason, the one with the fresh haircut enthusiastically said, "Come travel with us. We can take turns riding the cycle and walking. It will be nice to have our barber along with us."

"No, thank you. It does sound like fun and we're tempted to tag along, but we don't have that much time on this vacation. I wish we could but perhaps we'll meet again someday. Gee, we're glad to have met you and wish you both much luck." After exchanging addresses and telephone numbers, Penny and Jane kissed their new friends on their cheeks and waved goodbye.

Chapter 13—Beware of
French Stewardesses

Jourdan picked Penny and Jane up in the lobby of their hotel at 7:30 p.m. that evening after phoning that he would be
late. He was dressed in dinner clothes. Penny and Jane wore
formals they had brought along just for an occasion like
this. Penny's dress was an emerald, strapless sheath with a
bouffant flare at the bottom. The dress fit so tightly that she
wiggled as she took the required small steps. If it weren't
for the flare at the bottom, she would have had to hop. She
had accessorized the dress with white gloves, green dangling
earrings and dyed to match heels.

Jane was dressed in her favorite sky blue chiffon that
swirled about her small frame and gave the impression of a
doll dressed with loving care.

"It does not matter of the hour because we will still have
plenty of time for dinner before the first show." Jourdan explained as they were seated in the car.

It was about 8:30 p.m. when they were shown into the
Lido club. They followed their host through a long, deeply
carpeted entrance hall lined with gold chairs. They passed a
circular bar on their left as they were shown to a table near
the stage which extended out into the audience. Jourdan ordered a bottle of champagne as the menus were handed to
each of them. "I suggest filet mignon because here is the
best in Paris."

"We will rely on your advice." Jane said, smiling at him as
she looked around the spacious nightclub.

Penny followed her gaze, while Jourdan ordered for them.
They were amazed to see so many men and women watching
them.

"You both look magnificent, as usual, and you can see that
half of the guests agree with me."

"Thank you, kind sir. Golly, this is a fabulous place, isn't
it Jane? I'm so glad we came."

Their champagne was placed before them. They began to sip as they told Jourdan about the two young fellows from Texas. He roared with laughter as they finished. Refilling their glasses, he urged them to drink more. Appetizers were served and the girls tackled them eagerly. The dinner courses were served for over an hour and half, with more champagne accompanying the elegant meal.

As the lights dimmed after 10 p.m., the show began. Penny and Jane were on the edge of their seats during the first half of the fast-paced show! After their initial embarrassment had worn away, they agreed they had never seen such beauty as when the nude show girls went through their graceful dances. They were thrilled as a water fountain with lights of many colors shining on it cascaded lively to the beat of the music. They held their breath as the dancers performed a gorgeous bathing scene under the fountain.

They chuckled as the comedians raced around the stage bantering with the cast and audience. Because they spoke little French, Jourdan translated everything for them. They laughed when the audience did, then after his translation, they laughed again.

Jourdan explained the showgirls were watched in private life like baby chicks by a mother hen and they led very quiet, sheltered lives. After intermission, during which time they sipped champagne, the show beauties again paraded. Some waltzed with feathers of different pastel colors, others danced in gay costumes with their breasts exposed, and others appeared completely nude.

The show lasted for over three enchanting hours. The evening ended all too soon although it was the wee hours of the morning when Jourdan escorted them back to their hotel. Jane left a call for them to be awakened at seven in order to take a tour that had been previously arranged. The operator had to ring their room several times.

"I don't think I can get out of bed today. Oh, my aching head." Penny buried her head under the pillow and came up only after Jane continued to shake her.

"Well hangover or not, we have to go, so get up. I feel just as miserable as you."

After breakfast rolls, marmalade and several cups of coffee, they were moving but neither Jane nor Penny looked nearly as pretty as the night before. Groaning, they climbed aboard a bus that was to take them to Versailles to see where Louis XIV had lived, and Malmaison, the home of Napoleon and Josephine. They were relieved when the long bus ride ended and trudged wearily behind the guide during the tour of Malmaison and its rich furnishings.

It was a long trip. The girls had very bad hangovers. The guide spoke in four languages, French, Italian, Spanish and English, using all four every time he pointed out anything of interest. He had the sort of voice that was always the same droning pitch with no expression and no change of tempo.

Penny whispered. "If he doesn't shut up soon, I'm going to throw something at him. He is about to drive me crazy, just stark, raving mad. Oh damn! I feel bad."

"I wish we had gotten more sleep last night and felt better. This is an excellent tour but all I can think of is getting back to our hotel."

The guide took them to a sidewalk cafe for lunch where they ordered cokes and sandwiches but the cokes had dirty specks and they wouldn't drink them. They didn't know what to drink. They had been told not to drink milk or water except in the hotels. They finally ordered some champagne and after drinking that, they felt somewhat better. The second half of the day went faster.

That night they went to bed early, real early. After a good night's rest they were eager for more sightseeing. Dressed in comfortable clothes, they went in and out of little shops, strolled along the Champs-Élysées, the banks of the Seine, saw the Louvre, took pictures from the Arc de Triomphe, visited Notre Dame and ended the day at the Eiffel Tower. Penny bought a silk shirt for Jody.

"You're gonna dress him so well that he's not gonna marry you. He's just gonna keep sending you on trips shopping for him."

"Let's face it roomie, he is handsome."

"You're prejudiced, Penny."

"I'm engaged. I'm lovely. I use Ponds."

"Don't entertain me, Penny." Jane groaned.

After calling Jourdan, thanking him for making their stay magnifique, they caught up on writing duty postcards to relatives, and went to bed early.

After finishing their packing the next morning and purchasing a bottle of Pernod Ricard, they checked out of the L'Hotel de la Rue de Bourgogne and took a taxi to the airline terminal in town. They checked in, had their baggage checked and were told where to go to catch the bus to ride to the terminal from Paris to where their flight would depart. Wandering around the station, they looked at souvenirs, purchased magazines and talked about the wonderful time in Paris.

Several announcements came over the loud speaker but they were not paying attention, anticipating that someone would fetch them for the bus ride. After some time had passed and no one had approached them, they went in search of their bus only to find it had departed. Now they were stranded and their baggage was headed toward the airport terminal. After trying to converse with a non-English speaking agent, Penny and Jane looked around for someone to help them. About that time an elderly porter with a broom in his hand and a smile on his crinkling ruddy features approached them.

"I overheard your conversation at the ticket counter and perhaps I can be of service. I speak English and the thing to do is find a taxi for you. Come with me and I will put you in one."

"Gee, we sure would appreciate it. We're lucky that you came along." Some of the worry lines left Penny's face as she spoke to the kind, old man.

He took them outside and hailed a cab. He told the driver to take them to the airport and stood on the curb waving his handkerchief until they were out of sight. The travelers caught their flight without further incident.

They had a stop in Milan, Italy for about four hours and spent the time sight-seeing. They visited the Basilica of Sant'Ambrogio and Sant'Eustorgio where they took pictures and enjoyed the short, but exciting tour of the churches.

Back at the airport, while waiting for the flight to Rome, they met a French stewardess who spoke several languages . . . seven to be exact. Her pixie face was set off by light brown, short curly hair. Her eyes were a hazel color with long, thick, dark eyelashes. Her upturned nose and smiling full lips kept the men watching her every movement. Genavieve said she was on vacation and going to Rome, so Penny and Jane invited her to join them. Accepting, the three boarded together for the flight to Roma, the Eternal City.

After checking into the hotel and having an extra bed added to their room for Genavieve, the three women walked around the city for awhile. Genavieve had some friends to see so she bid them so long for awhile. After she left, they got in a taxi to ride around town and see some more sights. The cab driver took them up along a twisting, winding mountainside and stopped the cab. He told them to get out and look over the wall surrounding the driveway. They walked to the edge and peeped into the night. Penny caught her breath. Below was the most beautiful sight she had ever seen—the old ruins of Rome casting shadows in the moonlight with the lights of the city in the distance beyond. Both young women held their breath. Finally, Penny broke the silent wonder.

"I swear if anyone were to move down there I would be completely convinced that we were living in olden times and that it was a Roman gladiator moving. This is the most wonderful thing that has ever happened to me, Jane. I could stand here forever."

She turned her head and gazed at the scenery below, and then her gaze wandered on toward the old coliseum in the background. She could imagine some poor soul in there with a lion and she could almost hear the crowd cheering. She was completely enchanted and got a little annoyed when Jane nudged her arm and said, "Let's go."

"Oh, Jane, just let me stand here until I die and I'll go happy. I love this place. Jody has got to see this, just like it is tonight."

The cab driver took them to a festive open-air cafe right beside the Coliseum and they had a typical Italian dinner of pasta. Afterwards it was getting late so they took another taxi back to the hotel, met Genavieve and told her what they had seen.

"You'd better get a good night's sleep because tomorrow I'm going to take you to do more sight-seeing than you ever dreamed possible in such a short time." Genavieve said.

True to her word, 6:00 a.m. Genavieve was shaking them awake. "Hurry, hurry and get dressed. We have much to see. I have already ordered breakfast. Vite, vite!" They were both muttering protests when the knock on their door sent them scurrying to the bathroom while Genavieve admitted a waiter with a large tray.

By 0700 they were on their way. That first day they visited and fed the pigeons in several small squares centered with statues, fountains with such musical names as Piazza San Petro and Piazza Navona . . . and Piazza de Spagna, Chiesa Nuova, Sant'Andrea della Valle, S. Maria Della Vittoria, Sant'Andrea della Fratte, and San Giovanni in Laterano. Genavieve knew her way around. She flew into Rome on her regular flights and was anxious for her new-found friends to see as much as possible on their short vacation.

The three adventurers staggered into their hotel room late that night and fell across their beds. Never had they seen so much or been so tired. Genavieve had only let them stop for a lunch break and a sandwich for dinner.

Again the next day she woke them early and took them to see the Renaissance palaces of Montecitoria, Progaganda Fid, Barberina and Doria palaces. She really made their trip complete because they would never have covered so much ground in such a short time.

That night she took them to the famous Trevi fountain where they tossed in their three coins and made their wishes. Penny wished to return to Rome with Jody.

The fountain was surrounded by Italians and tourists, the women in gay colored summer blouses and full skirts. There were many couples holding hands and watching the fountain cascade. It was a romantic sight and both Jane and Penny were envious because they did not have loved one with them. They took several photos with a flash camera, and then Genavieve suggested they walk back to the hotel and look at some of the other fountains on the way. Again, Penny was totally enchanted with Rome.

The next day was spent leisurely. Genavieve was away with old friends and Penny and Jane were glad of a reprieve from her hectic tour pace. They were writing post cards that evening when Genavieve burst in announcing they were going to visit some night clubs with a friend of hers.

A short, dark haired young man named Antoine escorted them to a place called 'La Biblioteca de Bouteilles' which when translated, meant the library of bottles! Along every wall in bookcases were thousands of bottles of various shapes, forms and colors. Most of the bottles were full of different kinds of wine. Antoine ordered drinks, then he and Genavieve moved to the dance floor. Two men came over and asked Penny and Jane to dance and they surprised themselves by accepting.

Later, approaching another place Antoine took them, the two Americans were surprised to hear rock-'n'-roll being played by a band. They were even more amazed as they were seated to see so many young couples on the floor dancing just as if they were in a nightclub in New York or at a high school gym dance with an Elvis recording blaring. Soon after they were seated, Antoine found two good-looking friends to dance with Penny and Jane who had the time of their lives.

When Antoine and Genavieve mentioned leaving, Penny was astonished to realize it was four in the morning. Thanking Antoine for a great last night in Rome, they picked up a bottle of champagne 'for the road' and the three polished it off as they completed packing while the sun rose.

At noon they began their trip to the Isle of Capri and Ischia, gardens of paradise. The bus took them to Naples where they had a fish lunch on the waterfront, then caught a boat to the Isle of Capri. On the boat trip, they passed the island of Sorrento and beyond Sorrento, the Amalfi coast. The view was magnificent.

Capri is a tremendous rock surrounded by little rocks, rich and luxuriant vegetation. Penny could not figure how it all grew and remained so beautiful. The weather was warm and balmy. A little resort village, built on the side and top of the mountain overlooked the water which was a soft light blue with traces of green reflecting the scene.

They took a taxi up the winding mountainside road and were soon settled in their rooms. Genavieve insisted on having a room of her own rather than double up with Penny and Jane. Their room had a small balcony from which they could see part of the island and the Mediterranean in the distance. After unpacking they took a tour of the little village near their hotel and purchased a few souvenirs with Genavieve translating prices for them.

That night in the hotel restaurant, Jane and Penny ordered spaghetti. Genavieve ordered a cut of meat they were not familiar with and it looked good. She offered them a bit and they took it, commented that it didn't taste too bad and made the mistake of asking what kind it was.

Genavieve answered, "Cat."

Jane and Penny swallowed hard, looked at one another, mumbled "Excuse me" and ran to their room.

The next morning, having recovered somewhat, they looked out their balcony at the refreshing scenery and saw below them Genavieve waving to come join her. She suggested the beach for the day and they accepted eagerly. They walked about two miles downhill, winding and twisting with the road until they came to a spot where Genavieve stopped.

"Here is where we'll go in swimming."

Penny protested. "But we didn't bring any clothes except fall things and neither of us has a swim suit."

"Oh, that's okay. Here you can go in without anything on. A lot of people go swimming in the nude. I am."

Jane was shocked. "We can't do that! At least I can't because I am much too bashful. You go ahead and we'll wait while you have a little swim if you want to."

Genavieve peeled off her clothes and jumped in. Penny and Jane perched atop a large rock formation. Genavieve was splashing and calling "come on." Penny relented. "Well, I can't take this heat any longer. I'm going in, but I'm going to keep on my panties and bra. Want to join me?"

"Yes, might as well. We haven't seen another soul since we've been here and no one will see us. Let's go."

They stripped off their peddle pushers down to underclothes and waded into the clear, sparkling Mediterranean. The three had a delightful time and stayed in until they began to feel a sun burn taking hold of their shoulders, then Jane suggested getting out. The others agreed and climbed out on the boulders to get dressed. As they were finishing, they heard clapping and whistling above them. They looked up high and on an overhanging cliff rock stood two teenage boys waving and whistling. Jane and Penny were mortified but Genavieve brushed it off. "Pay no attention to them. You'll probably never see them again anyway."

They ignored the boys and soon they quit whistling and left. The three women then caught a mini-bus back up the hill to their hotel.

That night, in the hotel restaurant, who should appear but the two boys who had watched them as they swam earlier that afternoon. They were waiters in the hotel and hurried over with water and silver, and impishly whispered. "You girls shouldn't go swimming in those white things you had on. They cover up too much." Penny and Jane blushed and ate their meal with guilty glances at the waiters.

The following morning Penny and Jane went in a small boat with two friends of Genavieve's to see the underwater caves, view the blue grotto and other interesting spots along the water's edge. They had to emphatically insist they were not in the mood to 'faire l'amour' with the escorts along the hidden beaches behind the caves.

Wandering into the village square in the early evening, Jane and Penny were surprised to encounter almost two hundred people just sitting and talking. Adapting quickly, they also sat and talked with some of the natives of the Isle of Capri.

With money almost gone and vacation time over, they bid farewell to Genavieve, packed and started the long homeward journey. Traveling many modes of transportation including a horse and buggy down the mountainside, a boat back to Naples, a train to Rome and an airplane to the good old United States of America, the young stewardesses were exhausted from almost twenty hours of traveling by the time they were seated on the flight home. After boarding they immediately fell asleep. It was supposed to be a non-stop flight to Belgium where they would make their last connection to New York. They landed and the steward woke them and told them to get off the plane. Penny roused sleepily and looked out the window. There was a sign outside that displayed Frankfurt Main.

"Jane! I believe we are in Germany."

Jane leaned across her and looked out the window at the sign. "Oh, no, goose. That's just an advertisement for a hot dog."

Penny shrugged her shoulders. "Well, if you say so."

They got off the plane with the rest of the passengers and were put in an open type bus similar to a trolley car and were driven to the terminal building which was surrounded with armed uniformed men.

Penny was fully awake by this time and as she took in the situation, she nudged Jane and whispered, "We are in Germany! Just look at the soldiers and the guns!"

"No, Penny, we are just at a different airport in Brussels and the reason the men are dressed like that is because it must be some kind of a holiday and they probably had a parade. Quit worrying and let's check on our flight to New York."

Penny glared at Jane but didn't say anything more about it as they walked into the building. The steward from the plane approached them and told them to go into the restaurant to eat, compliments of the airline.

Penny leaned over toward the table next to theirs and asked an English couple that had been on their flight what was going on. They explained that they had to land in Germany due to bad weather in Brussels and would wait there until it cleared. Penny whirled around to face Jane. "Don't tell me anything else. You don't know any more than I do and right now you don't know as much."

Finding seats in the lobby, they settled in to people watch. They were too tired to do any sightseeing and were anxious to be on their way home. The minutes ticked slowly as only they can when someone is sitting in an airport waiting to go home. After waiting for five hours, they heard the announcement that their flight was ready to depart. When they reached Brussels it was a race to clear customs and they barely made their connection to New York.

They were homeward bound at last and almost immediately upon takeoff, Penny fell into another sound sleep. Jane was restless so she picked up a magazine and went to the lounge to read. When Penny woke, several of the people around her asked if she was alright and did she feel okay. She couldn't understand their concern and asked, "Why? Did I yell in my sleep or talk too much?"

One matronly blue-haired woman smiled and replied, "Why, my dear, you haven't moved a muscle or turned for several hours and we were wondering if you had died."

Reaching their apartment in the wee hours, they dug for a door key and once inside dropped their things with a thud screaming in unison, "Gosh, it's good to be home!"

Jody had missed Penny so much during her trip to Europe that he pressed for an early wedding date. Having had her flight, she complied. She wrote her letter of resignation and began the last two weeks of a career that she thoroughly enjoyed.

Having had several unusual episodes in her flying days it was only fitting that her very last flight would present the unexpected.

The DC-7 was revving up the engines on the end of the runway for takeoff. Everyone was buckled in. Suddenly a large woman with two small children clutching each hand being pulled along behind the woman and a diaper bag trailing started running down the aisle from the forward cabin yelling, "Stop! Stop!"

Penny quickly unfastened her own seat belt and met the woman midway in the cabin aisle. The woman was almost hysterical. Her eyes were wide with terror and her yelling had an unnatural pitch to its urgency. The engines were reaching their capacity.

Penny tried to hold the huge, shaking woman but was ineffective against her surge toward the door beyond the buffet area. Both children were crying. A man stood near the spot and tried to help hold the woman. Halting her momentarily, she screamed at Penny. "I's getting off! I's getting off! I's getting off dis airplane now. I's ain't flying! I's can't!" She surged forward, knocking Penny aside. She reached the buffet door and started struggling with the large handle in the center of the massive door. Penny tried to get between the woman and the door. Managing to put her body in front of the woman, Penny flipped the emergency call button to the cockpit. The other stewardess was trying to pull the woman from the door. The plane rolled smoothly into takeoff position. Penny clicked the emergency call button. The captain's voice boomed. "What's wrong?"

Penny yelled into the Mike. "A passenger is opening the door"

"Get them away from that door!"

"Captain, I can't! I need help!"

"We're taking off! We're cleared for takeoff!"

The woman gave a desperate shove, knocking Penny aside. She unlatched the lock position of the handle. The warning signal flashed in the cockpit. The captain, now aware of the emergency taxied the giant bird off the takeoff runway, notifying the control tower they had door open warning light flashing and that he were returning to the gate. Penny, recovering her balance, grabbed the woman's muscular brown arm. "Please, please calm down! We're going back. Don't open the door. I said, do not open the door!"

For the first time the woman was aware of Penny holding onto her. She blinked her frightened eyes. "I's ain't going! I's can't! I's can't fly! I's sorry but I's ain't going."

"Please return to your seat with your two children. We will take you back to the terminal. Please go to your seat." She flipped the switch signaling the cockpit calling.

"Alright Penny. What in the hell is going on back there?" the captain's voice bellowed.

"We've got a petrified woman passenger. She refuses to go and she's cracked the handle of the door. We've got to take her back to the terminal."

Penny left wedding preparations to her mother. Two days before her wedding, she and Jane traveled together from Atlanta to Lubbock where Jane, as maid of honor, helped her goose of a roommate lasso a new roommate for life.

The Sixties

Airline stewardesses are very special people.

They are the 'people pleasers'. Poised, attractive people who like people! These are the young women who make the grade as airline stewardesses. It is not an easy job . . . not all fun and glamour. The rewards are many for the woman who can qualify, who wants to develop her personality and appearance, and to widen her horizons.

She is one in 100!

As an airline stewardess, you will meet many interesting people from all walks of life. Your manner, your thoughtfulness, your ability to make their trip more pleasant will carry your image to the traveling public.

Can you qualify?

If you are the one woman in 100 who has these qualities and can say "yes" to the following questions, there is a rewarding career waiting for you.

1. Are you single, never been married?
2. Is your appearance neat, attractive, your complexion clear?
3. Do you have a friendly personality and high moral character?
4. Are you in good health?
5. Have you good vision, or have you been wearing contact lenses successfully for six months, with uncorrected vision of at least 20/30 with no astigmatism? (Glasses are not permitted.)
6. Are you a high school graduate with two years of college or equivalent business experience?
7. Are you between 20 and 26 years of age?

8. Are you 5' 2" to 5' 8" tall in stocking feet?
9. Is your weight in proportion to your height and not more than 135 pounds?
10. Do you like to travel?

If you meet our qualifications, we will arrange a personal interview with you.

Chapter 14—Two Dry Martinis and One Wheelchair

"One important reason for stewardesses to be aboard aircraft is safety. When an emergency situation arises at 40,000 feet, passengers have nobody to turn to except stewardesses. It is an awesome responsibility for a young woman. Are there any audience questions?"

Linda Schuyler, tall, with shiny, straight, chin-length hair beneath her chartreuse trimmed beige pillbox hat, stood at a speaker's podium in front of a career seminar at Boston University. She was in Southaire's bright new stewardess 880 jet uniform and was on special assignment recruiting prospective 'people pleasers'.

A raised hand was acknowledged. "Does your airline have female pilots?" A giggle followed the squeaky tone.

Linda detested questions obviously designed to draw attention to the questioner. She thought, *how am I supposed to answer a question like that? What does it have to do with being a stew anyway?* She thrust a sickeningly sweet smile in the direction of the tittering sounds. "No. Not yet. When it is feasible for the continuing success of Southaire, you can be assured women will pilot the aircraft. If there are no further questions, I'll continue."

Linda squinted toward the blurring beige faces. She admonished herself. You're getting tired, girl. You're pushing yourself too hard, shouldn't have signed up for special assignments. I better see the eye doc soon as I get home. It's probably time for a prescription change on the contacts. She straightened her shoulders. Although she had a reference notebook on the podium, Linda preferred extemporaneous speaking.

"Today's stews lead very interesting lives, are active in worthwhile projects and do quite a bit of volunteer work. All the negative things you hear nowadays about stewardesses are, for the most part, wrong and they don't bother anyone connected with the profession. Those same kinds of things can be said about any group of women. Women of today have the greatest opportunity imaginable to meet the most remarkable people of a decade. All the people you read about or hear about on television, the news makers, fly on airplanes and stewardesses get to meet them. We associate with headliners daily. That's a nice benefit to this job. A smart woman can do her job like she's supposed to, take advantage of the benefits offered through the airline, broaden her mind by traveling and capitalize on her experiences the rest of her life. As a stewardess we play many rolls—a diplomat when 196 passengers show up for a stretch DC-8 that holds 195 . . . a maître-d when we have to serve dinner to that 195 load with 187 prepared meals . . . a kindergarten teacher to handle unaccompanied minors . . . a nurse to comfort the air sick first rider . . . a psychologist to sooth the inevitable drunk . . . and if he can't be quieted, then we have to assume the roll of policeman. Through all these routine situations, we have to be a safety officer and a public relations representative for Southaire. If you think you can accept this sort of responsibility, then Southaire will be pleased to look over your application. Material is available on the table in the rear of this auditorium."

A heavy-set blonde with an oversized beehive hair style stood and asked shyly, "I always thought stewardesses had to be beautiful?"

Linda laughed and assumed her best bathing beauty pose. "You mean I'm not your idea of a movie star?" The person who had asked quickly sat down blushing all the way up to the roots of her outlandish hairdo.

Linda said, "Seriously, that was a good question. The old idea of a glamour gal in the sky isn't practical or fair. We do have physical requirements, but they are based mostly on health, and a pleasing appearance. We all want to look as good as we can." She laughed and put her hands on her sturdy hips, and added, "Some of us have to try harder than others."

Mrs. Warrack, a faculty member at the university, rushed to Linda as she stepped away from the podium. "Thank you so much for coming and speaking at our little seminar, Miss Schuyler. We all learned so much. You certainly do a good job selling Southaire."

"Well, that's my job."

Within a few hours Linda, who left behind the Boston cool autumn, stepped into the late summer mugginess of Atlanta. As she was checking her message box in the stewardess lounge, the chief stewardess, Sue, turned from her paperwork and smiled. "How did it go in Boston? Did you get us some new recruits?"

"I just might have." Linda squinted at Sue's round face.

"You're pooped, my girl," said Sue. "I can always tell by your eyes. I hope you'll have a good rest before your next flight."

"That depends on whether you call ten hours a good rest. I've got the 0845 L.A. flight in the morning."

The next day Linda made her seat count and had eight empties. She reported to the agent, knowing that there were more than a dozen soldier standbys to fill the empty seats. She hated to have to leave the men behind when there was no more room. Their eager eyes and young innocent expressions tugged at her heart, especially when she knew this trip was taking them one step closer to the horror of Vietnam.

In a few minutes, every seat loaded, the temperamental, intricate 880 was sweeping the sky, leaving far below the noise and the first surge of power on takeoff. Linda loved the Convair 880 aircraft. Reaching a 35,000 feet leveling-off cruise, she was again reminded of the passenger who told her, "An 880 flight is as close as I'll ever get to a ride in a fighter plane. I love the gut feeling I get every time the landing gear slams up into the fuselage."

An elderly couple stopped Linda before she reached the buffet area. "Will you please arrange to have a wheelchair for my husband in Los Angeles?" The aging beauty in the window seat leaned across the man seated beside her. "Jack's arthritis is acting up terribly and even though he denies needing one, I know a wheelchair will make it easier for us to get through the airport."

She smiled proudly. "We're on our way to Honolulu for a honeymoon. We've been married 58 years and decided it's high time to take the honeymoon of our dreams. And could you please bring us martinis, very dry, when you start serving?"

Linda grinned. "Two dry martinis and one wheelchair coming up".

During the meal service Linda went ahead of the food serving stewardess helping set up trays and preparing passengers for lunch.

A boy about 12 years old, traveling alone, who was trying very hard to act grown-up, stopped Linda at his seat. "Miss, I'll have a cheeseburger and a coke."

Suppressing a laugh, she explained. "I'm sorry, I can give you a coke, but we don't have any cheeseburgers on board. You see our food is prepared on the ground and put on the plane in hot ovens. Then we take the hot food and put it on trays just before we serve, but we don't actually do any cooking. So, I'm sorry but I can't bring you a cheeseburger."

Undaunted, he looked her in the face and replied in his best adult manner. "That's okay. It's not your fault. I'll settle for a plain hamburger."

Just before landing in L.A., Linda noticed a fragile young woman, holding a sleeping baby, sobbing uncontrollably. Linda knelt in the aisle beside the woman's seat. "Can I be of some help? Would you like me to hold your baby while you go to the ladies room?"

Through hankie-muffled sobs the young woman nodded. Linda took the snoozing baby and walked up and down the aisle until the mother returned. As she was seated, she nervously explained. "My husband has had a heart attack. He was in California on business. We just moved from Greenville, South Carolina to Marietta, Georgia last week. Everything is still half-way packed. I don't know any of my neighbors. We have no family near us. Things were already in turmoil and now this—my husband Ray out on the West coast with a heart attack."

Her green eyes started misting over. "Ray has never had heart trouble. I can't believe this is happening. When the Los Angeles Mercy Hospital called, I thought it was a horrible mistake. I just grabbed up Gretchen, got on this flight and here we are. I don't know what's going to happen. I don't mean to cry. I've been trying to hold back. Ray's in intensive care."

The baby was sucking on its fingers and cooing blissfully. Linda's heart went out to the young mother. "Our limo goes right by L.A. Mercy Hospital. Would you like to ride with us? I'm sure my crew won't mind."

"Oh, miss, that would be so nice. I've never felt more alone or been so frightened in all my life." The young woman started crying again.

Linda patted her quivering shoulder. "I'll help you all I can. Let's fasten in you and your baby. Did you say, uh, Gretchen?"

"Yes, Gretchen. You're very kind."

"We're almost landing. Remain in your seat and after the rest of the passengers get off, I'll help you and Gretchen."

Linda busied herself with pre-landing and embarkment duties. As soon as she could, she hurried to assist the frightened young woman. When the Southaire crew limo stopped at L.A. Mercy Hospital, Linda alighted to continue to help the young mother with her baby as long as she was needed.

On the return flight to Atlanta, a heavily rouged, flashy looking woman rushed up to Linda. "I dropped my diamond wedding band into the lavatory. Do something!"

"I can't do anything in the air, but after we land, I'll try to get someone to help."

"I have to get it back! This is my second marriage and my husband will be terribly upset. I mean I'm upset too, don't get me wrong, but my second husband is jealous of my first husband and I still have my first wedding ring and it's a beautiful thing, four carats of diamonds, and my husband will swear I threw this one away just so I could use the first one again and that's not true." She grabbed Linda's arm. "Do something!"

Linda was tired. She had been up most of the night baby sitting the child of the young woman they had helped get to the hospital. The young father died at two AM then Linda had helped the panic stricken young widow make calls and get a room at the crew hotel for the night. Linda had wearily fallen into bed at 0600 only to have to get up for 0800 crew call. Now she was facing this wild-eyed creature that had lost her ring. Linda's thoughts were not public relations thoughts. *You nincompoop, you should never take off a ring in a public place, especially a moving public place that is subject to a bounce at any moment.* She pulled her arm away and rubbed the spot where the lady's fingernails had dug into her skin.

"As soon as we land, I'll report it and Southaire's personnel will do their best to recover your ring for you. Please return to your seat. We'll be serving champagne in just a few minutes."

Linda gave the woman a friendly but forceful nudge toward the seat and said emphatically, "We'll be serving in just a few seconds."

As she walked back towards the buffet, Linda muttered to herself. "After flights like this, I doubt that I can ever again tell groups of women how rewarding it is to be a people pleaser!"

The following day Linda's alarm clock woke her at 0800 after a sound night's sleep in her own bed. It took her a few moments to recall why she had wanted to rise at such an ungodly hour on her day off.

She hopped out of her warm bed when she remembered her promise to the Inner City Foundation to be the coordinator of the volunteer painting crew that was going to try to turn a decaying old house in the heart of the city into a cheerful day nursery for underprivileged children. She donned a

faded North Carolina State football jersey and paint splattered jeans. Her usually brief beauty regime was reduced to a
quick splash of warm water on her face and her hair brushed
up into a wispy ponytail. Not even pausing for breakfast,
Linda maneuvered her temperamental blue Volkswagen toward the deteriorating heart of the city. Linda's surroundings changed to slums. As she looked out the car windows
she couldn't help thinking *why are there so many uncaring
people? Atlanta's a beautiful city, historic, religious . . . and
yet something like this happens. No one seems to care. They
seem to be more concerned with selfish material acquisi-
tions than with helping others. God gives you the ability to
create and build a town like Atlanta and then people don't
appreciate what we have. Nobody wants to work together.*
As she drove through the bumpy and worn streets, she shook
her head sadly at the wasted crumbling buildings that had
once been beautiful, artistic creations.

When she pulled up in front of the defeated looking house,
she wondered again why she was involved with this project.
What good can my efforts do anyone? I can't change the
world all by myself. Am I just kidding myself that I'm doing
good for some people?

A plump, middle aged woman, her warm brown face reflecting confusion, met Linda halfway up the walk. "Linda,
I'm so glad you're here. A whole bunch of teen volunteers
just arrived and they're in there arguing and running around".
Mrs. Amy Jackson's usual calm was deserting her. "There's
one fellow that wants to paint the front room yellow and another guy's slapping on green like there's no tomorrow."

Linda squared her shoulders and marched through the
front door. A two-fingered whistle, taught to her by her big
brother, brought order to the chaos of paintbrush-waving
young men and women. "Look folks, your group volunteered to help fix up this old house, not completely destroy
it. If you didn't come here to work, you can go home now.
This paint was donated and we don't have the money to buy
more, so let's not waste it."

Her face softened at the embarrassed looks on the faces of the youthful group. "Mrs. Amy Jackson is the director of the day nursery and she'll tell you which color goes where. I'll assign two of you to each room, and then we'll get cracking. There's a lot of work to do."

Within a few minutes everyone was diligently working on an assigned wall. The loudest sound in the house was the musical urging of Chubby Checker to 'twist again' pouring from a portable radio.

Linda and Amy Jackson sat at a small metal table in the kitchen sipping coffee and making plans.

"I won't be able to come in again until Sunday afternoon, but the fabric I talked Prices into donating should be here by then and we can start on the curtains."

"Linda, we're happy to have anything you can give us. There aren't many young people willing to give up their time off like this. I hope you know how grateful we are."

Linda smiled shyly and quickly changed the subject with a direct question. "What other groups do you think we can call for Volunteer action?"

It was nearly dark before Linda eased her aching body into the driver's seat of her Volkswagen, Brunhilde. She realized for the first time that busy day that she was famished. As the turned the key in the ignition she spoke to her little car, "Okay, Brunie, don't give me any trouble. I want to go home and get something to eat."

A whining buzz was the only answer she received. As she stepped on the clutch and fiercely turned the key again, Linda demanded, "Start, darn it, I'm in no mood for one of your temper tantrums." With a cough and a sputter the engine caught and began to hum.

Pulling away from the curb Linda thought, *that's one more win for me but I wonder how long Brunhilde is going to last.* The streetlight illuminated the faded pink brick facade of Linda's apartment house. Deep shadows darted among the ivy that laced over the walls. It was an older building, lacking in some of the more modern conveniences but Linda liked the large rooms, thick walled privacy and the luxury of her own fireplace.

As she stepped into the entrance way which led to the one flight of stairs to her apartment, Linda saw a figure seated on the dimly lit stairs. *Old Mr. Caughlin has had too much to drink again*, she thought. The figure rose, unfolding what seemed like endless arms and legs. His tall backlit body in its rumpled suit looked like a friendly scarecrow.

"Tom! What are you doing here?" Linda exclaimed.

"Hi, Linda. I knew you were spending the day at the day nursery so I figured you might like some dinner and a dull dinner companion." He held out a cardboard bucket of fried chicken.

"You dull? Never! I'm the one who's about as interesting as a cabbage tonight. But what a starving cabbage!" She grabbed the bucket and raced up the stairs. "Last one to my door gets the wings."

Loping past her two steps at a time Tom accepted the challenge. "You're on!"

Chapter 15—Birds, Pollution, and Routine Coffee Breaks

After two days off duty and plenty of rest, Linda was her usual, well-controlled self on a flight from Chicago to Dallas. The super 727 was cruising at 580 miles per hour. The four stewardesses were in the middle of a meal service when a man's terrified voice shrieked, "Don't touch me! What are you doing to me? Help! Help! They're trying to get me!"

Being the nearest stewardess, Linda quickly handed her tray of beverages to a passenger in the aisle seat and rushed toward the bellowing male voice.

"Don't let them get me. Please help me, puleeessseeeesss." A bearded, middle-aged man was thrashing in his seat. The lady next to him, frightened speechless, had crawled as far down on the floor under the seat as she could get. Linda tried to touch the man's shoulder but he was thrashing around too much for her to make contact.

One of her helper stews appeared and Linda hurriedly told her, "Continue the meal service. My tray's somewhere back there. I think I can handle this okay if I can just get his attention." She tried to make the man hear her voice over his own hollering. "Hey, hey, mister, what is it?"

"Don't touch me! They're trying to get me!" He turned pleading, bloodshot eyes in her direction. "Officer, officer, help me! They're coming from all directions."

Trying to break into his brief span of attention, Linda reached a hand forward and said, "I'm here. I'll help you. They won't get you. Try to relax."

He grabbed her arm and yanked her. Linda had to put her knee in his lap to keep from falling. Hugging her arm to his face, he whimpered. "Oh, please, please, please, please, don't let them get me, don't let them get me, don't let . . ."

Halting another serving stew, Linda asked her to bring a cold wet cloth and a cup of water.

The man was now sobbing and clutching Linda's arm as he would a life preserver. Linda managed to twist her body around enough to sit on the arm of the seat. Thinking him calm enough, she motioned for the crouching woman in the window seat to squeeze by them and into the aisle. Still too shocked to speak, the trembling woman nodded and began slowly moving over. As she was attempting to climb over the distraught man's legs, he saw her moving toward him and started another thrashing and screaming seizure.

A burley passenger seated behind them stood up and grabbed the petrified woman. He lifted her over the seat and put her gently down into the vacant seat beside him. He talked to her until her nerves were calmed.

The stewardess brought the cold cloth and Linda tried to place it at the nape of the bearded man's neck to calm him. Feeling the cold, he stopped tossing and whirled toward Linda with both fists. She pulled back avoiding a blow. "Take it easy, I'm trying to help."

With his fists in front of him in a fighters pose, the man blinked his eyes several times as if fighting to come out of his nightmare.

The other stewardess' voices could be heard. "Please return to your seats. Stop blocking the aisle. Everyone be seated!"

Linda reached gently forward and encased the man's fists with her own small hands. "Try to relax. No one is going to hurt you. What is your name?"

With fists clenched and a glassy stare, he muttered, "Marvin."

"Put your hands down, Marvin. Put them in your lap! I have some water for you. I'll hold the glass for you, Marvin. Put your hands in your lap. Now sip, easy, easy. Relax. Sip the water."

While the passengers deplaned in Dallas, Linda stayed with Marvin. An agent came to assist and she went through elaborate introductions of the agent to Marvin to maintain a sense of calm for the troubled passenger. Together, she and the agent got Marvin into Southaire's Operations Manager's office. Then they coaxed his billfold from him for identification and managed to understand from his incoherent mumbling the name of a relative in Dallas.

When they contacted the cousin, he refused to come to the airport for Marvin. Local police were called. Marvin again went into panic with everyone except Linda. Realizing she was the only one he trusted, Linda volunteered to ride with the police to take Marvin to Parkland Hospital in Dallas.

Southaire released Linda from her return flight duties, and she and the Southaire agent accompanied the distraught Marvin to emergency and gave the cousin's name as the nearest relative.

Linda and the agent stayed at the hospital until Marvin was sedated and resting in the Psychiatric wing. They were having coffee in the hospital cafeteria when one of the police officers joined them.

"Well, we finally got some kind of story from the cousin."

"I just can't understand him not wanting to help Marvin," Linda said angrily.

"It seems that this isn't the first time Marvin's pulled something like this. His cousin said that he's been emotionally ill for a long time, but he lives with his mother and she refused to get him medical help."

"He's always taking his mother's credit cards and flying all over the country trying to get some relative or another to protect him from the Communists."

"The Communists?" The agent looked incredulous.

"That's right. His cousin said that Marvin hasn't been right since he got back from a Korean P.O.W. camp ten years ago. The cousin says he is getting transferred to a Veteran's hospital where he will finally get help."

On New Year's Day, Linda was scheduled for a 0640 departure and a ten-hour duty day. Wanting to start the New Year off right, she spent the party night at home getting a good night's sleep.

At 0440 the wake-up call came from crew scheduling. Since her old blue Volkswagen, Brunhilde, was being over-hauled, Linda phoned for a cab for 0530, only to be told there would be a two-hour delay in cabs unless she could be ready in 15 minutes to share one that was already in her neighbor-hood. Frantically she put on uniform, threw luggage together and was pulling curlers out of her hair when the cab's horn sounded.

With curlers half in and half out, no nylons or make-up on, and hairpiece in hand, Linda arrived at crew scheduling. She stepped out of the cab, and promptly slipped on the ice, falling on her back and dumping the contents of her luggage all over the pavement.

Embarrassed, but relieved that no one was around to see her, she picked herself up, gathered her things and walked into crew scheduling hoping it would be empty. The entire crew of six people sat in the lobby.

As Linda passed by them, everyone stopped talking and stared at her. The silence was broken by the captain saying "Wow! She must really know how to celebrate New Year's Eve!"

The day got no better as Linda served groaning New Year's Eve celebrants who were suffering from gigantic hangovers. She had hurt her back when she fell on the ice and it was throbbing. Her thoughts plagued her as she prepared a tray of Bloody Marys. *I must be in the wrong job. Sometimes I can't stand people. If one more foul smelling clod paws at me today and suggests I hold his ailing head, I'm gonna give him something to suffer from.*

Finishing with the serving routine, Linda strolled through the cabin and exchanged tired smiles with her counterpart who was passing magazines. Linda made a smoking gesture to the other stewardess, then slipping into the cockpit, she quickly lit a cigarette. The crew was busy and only briefly acknowledged her. She stood behind the flight engineer and looked beyond the instrument panel into the flawless New Year's Day of 1965. *What mysteries do you hold bright and beautiful New Year? What plans do I have that you will put asunder? What discoveries will be tremendous this year? What inventions? What miracles?*

A few days later, Linda and two other stewardesses boarded passengers on a super DC-9 for the Atlanta to Newark flight. It was a fully booked short run, and the three stewardesses had to move in swift precision to keep the tight schedule on this popular flight.

A good-looking guy stopped Cynthia as she was checking seat belts. "Did you happen to notice a belt on the steps or in the aisle?"

"No sir. But I'll look as soon as I have a chance."

When Virginia, who was placing articles in the overhead rack, approached the man, he again inquired. "Did you find a belt anyplace around?"

"Nope, sorry. But I'll look as soon as I have time."

Linda was in the middle of flight origination announcements concerning oxygen, safety procedures and the seat belt warning sign, when a male passenger ran by her. Startled, she turned to watch as he ran to the front of the plane and started rummaging through the coat closet. As everyone looked on in wonderment, his pants suddenly fell to the floor.

Standing there in full view of the cabin's occupants in only his sport shirt and underwear, he coolly turned to his surprised audience. After casting an 'I asked you first' glance at stewardesses Cynthia and Virginia, he asked the passengers in a composed manner, "has anybody seen my belt?"

In the middle of a lazy Wednesday morning, Linda received a phone call from a pilot friend who shared her last name—Schuyler. "Hey, Linda Schuyler, this is your namesake, Art Schuyler. I've got a guy here with me in Operations who wants to meet you. He saw you breeze through a while ago when you got off 327 and he won't go home till he's been introduced. I made the mistake of telling him I knew you. Whatcha say? Wanna crack a beer with us? We'll either bring some, or pick ya up and go to my place."

"C'mon over here, Namesake. I think there's beer in the fridge, if not we'll drink coffee."

"Yuck! Coffee at ten in the morning!"

"Schuyler, some day I have to tell you about the birds, pollution and routine coffee breaks."

"You'll like Mike. It'll be the match of the air world. I'll get to give the bride away. Cupid is my name, love is my game."

"Yawn! I can hardly wait."

Art Schuyler and Mike McPherson arrived cradling a six pack of Coors beer. Schuyler thrust it at Linda. "Best beer in the Southwest cause ya can't get it anyplace else. Mike and I brought in a case on cargo this morning."

"You could get fired if you get caught. Southaire won't appreciate you being a beer runner."

"Mike won't tell. I won't tell, and I'll kill you if you do. So we're safe."

"Come on in. Nestling the beer, she stuck out one hand to shake. "Hi, Mike. Welcome."

"Good to meet you, Linda. It's nice of you to let us come over."

During their hour visit, Linda managed a serious conversation with McPherson amidst trading quips with Schuyler. She was surprised to learn Mike was the son of Senator Phil McPherson.

When he asked her for a date, she accepted eagerly. She was as interested in the flamboyant politician father as she was in the copilot son.

Linda's next flight was a computer company charter to Caracas. Normally the run was held by the most senior stewardesses of Southaire, but Linda was a requested stew for the special holiday charter because she had previously taken part in an advertising promotional movie and was well liked by the computer executives.

When she checked in at the stewardess department, Sue, her supervisor, beckoned. "Linda, come in my office for a couple of minutes."

Knowing she had done nothing wrong, Linda relaxed in a chair in front of Sue's desk.

"Linda, you know huge corporations spend thousands of dollars to get their customers in a room for one day so the company can present its product. The airline industry does it every day when that door is closed on a flight full of people."

Sue smiled as Linda nodded. "When airline customers are closed up in a small area the airlines put on a show. It's done every flight. It's been done since the origination of steward-esses and it always will be done. Those customers are a cap-tive audience. It's up to the stewardesses to create an image of the airline. You were requested for this charter. Therefore, you're even more on display, not only during the flight but for the entire three days you're in Caracas. This company is a tremendous account for Southaire."

"I understand, Sue. I'm honored to have been chosen and you know I'll do my best for Southaire."

Linda routinely glanced through her airline mail, checked her schedule and read the bulletin board before boarding. On board, the copilot handed her the tabs sheet for estimated time of departure and estimated time of arrival. She added it to her clipboard which already contained flight reports, count sheets, cleaning ducats, emergency forms and night pay sheets.

Once the buffet check was completed, the three stews went on with their pre-flight audit of medicine kit, lavatory supplies, oxygen containers, magazines, pillows, blankets, entertainment kit of cards, chess and checkers, coat hangers, coat tags, and their jump seat oxygen masks. When the 92 company officials and their wives were settled aboard the Convair 880, Linda signed the agent's form transferring re-sponsibility for the passengers from his ground domain over to her cabin accountability.

The breath-taking acceleration of the powerful Convair 880 as it climbed for level flight altitude alarmed a few of the wives, and the stew call buttons signaled summons from anxious husbands.

Drinks were quickly passed, followed by hors d'oeuvres. As a more calm mood settled over the vacationers, Linda and her two co-attendants mingled with the passengers to visit and attend to even the simplest wishes.

Over the shimmering blue water between Cuba and Jamaica, the airplane began to wobble, disrupting the tranquility of the perfect flight. The nose of the 880 yawed port and starboard in a drunken, un-coordinated condition. The cabin was thrown into turmoil. Even before the lights flashed, Linda was on the intercom while the other two stews began making people fasten seat belts. "Please fasten your seat belts immediately. There is no danger. We have encountered either turbulence or our plane is in a situation called 'A Dutch roll'. Either way, your crew is perfectly equipped to take care of the situation."

Almost before she replaced the mike, the ship was into a climbout and leveling at a smoother altitude. Making a cabin check, Linda was startled to hear music at a seat where a couple were leaning back with their eyes closed. Halting at their seat, she looked closer. In between them was a portable radio. Knowing the signals from portables may interfere with navigation instruments, she tried to lean over the man to turn it off.

As she flipped the switch, he opened his eyes and grabbed her hand. "What are you doing?"

His hand still grasped her wrist and she was frozen in a leaning position with her face very close to his. "I'm so sorry to wake you. I was just turning off your radio."

"Why? I want it on."

"I'm sorry sir, but the signals from your radio reflect in the cockpit. Would you let go of my wrist, please? I'm getting a back ache in this position."

Ramming his seat straight, he uttered, "Preposterous! I never heard such gobbledygook."

"It's hard to explain. I'm sorry but radios being played in flight are forbidden."

"I don't believe you. Let me talk with your Captain." He started to rise.

His wife, fully awake, tugged at his coat sleeve. "Honey, it's okay. We don't need to play our radio." She smiled at Linda. "Perhaps you would be good enough to bring us some coffee, dear."

"Certainly. I'm truly sorry about the radio, but rules are . . ."

The angry man interrupted by standing and moving into the aisle. "I'm going to the cockpit."

Knowing one minor upset could put a damper on such a special charter, Linda was concerned. There was no hesitation on her part to follow safety rules, but she must now cool a hot-headed passenger. "I'll be delighted to take you to the cockpit, sir, but first it must be cleared with the Captain. Please have a seat while I contact him on the intercom."

The man turned to his wife. 'See, you just have to be firm with hired subordinates. I'll get this matter cleared at once. You just relax, my dear, and I'll soon have your music going again."

Standing beside him, Linda felt a strong desire to practice her judo on Mr. Bigshot. Clenching her teeth to gain control, she lowered voice. "If you don't want to sit, you can stroll a bit while I call the cockpit."

"I'll go with you. I want to hear what you say."

"As you wish."

When she hung up, she said, "Captain Carlsen suggests you bring your radio with us."

Inside the cockpit, the engineer offered the man his seat. Linda winked her thanks at Captain Carlsen and retreated, closing the door.

As Linda was checking seat belts for landing and handing down personal belongings from the overhead rack, the man with the radio stopped her.

"My dear, I owe you a sincere apology. Your very nice captain illustrated to me radio interference. You've taught me a very practical lesson—when people are hired to do a job, let them do their job. You are very capable. How would like to work for my company?"

Smirking, Linda looked him straight in his apologetic eyes. "I believe I am already working for your company and have this whole flight."

Venezuelan folktales, called gaitas navidenas, performed by groups of people singing about happenings of past and present, heightened the sunny mood of the charter passengers as they entered the Caracas terminal in Venezuela.

The three-day holiday included a breathtaking series of sights including bright modern buildings accented with orange, yellow and bright blue. A cable car trip up a mountainside to a dining room on its summit above witnessed swirling cloud puffs. And sounds assaulted them above and warm breezes played about as they swayed to the tango and cha-cha rhythms floating in the night. They felt the beat of the furros drums, the thunk of the stick-like tamboresi, the soft guitar strum of cuatros and the hollow rattle of maracas at the colorful small night clubs teeming with happy visitors to this enchanting place.

All too soon for everyone, the holiday was over, and once again the Convair 880 was slamming its landing gear up into the fuselage.

Chapter 16—He'd look Stunning
in Pink Chiffon

Linda dressed with special care for her first date with Mike McPherson. He had gotten front row tickets to a big Broadway musical comedy road production that was presenting a one-night performance at the local community theater.

Before she had finished with her make-up, the doorbell rang. In dismay, Linda checked her watch. "He's not supposed to be here for twenty minutes. I hope I haven't gotten myself mixed up with an early bird," she muttered as she went to answer the insistent chiming.

"Hi kid! Wow! What are you all dolled up for?" Tom slipped through the narrow door opening and flopped, as if to stay, on the sofa.

"Believe it or not, I've got a date." She made an exaggerated pose and pronounced in haughty tones, "To the thee-ate-tah and late dinner, my deah."

Bunching the silver and green silk folds of her cocktail dress beneath her, Linda curled up on the sofa next to her friend.

"I'm sorry that I'm busy. Did you have something special you wanted to do tonight? Or did you just come over to clean out my refrigerator and waste my time again?"

"What ya got in your fridge?"

"Tom!" She started to get up.

"I'm kidding. Sit down. I just want to fill you in on the latest in the Jameson murder case."

They were engrossed in Tom's case and Linda was startled when the doorbell chimed. She jumped guiltily from the sofa. "Oh, my gosh. That's my date. His name is Mike McPherson. He's a pilot. Entertain him while I finish my make-up." She dashed for her bedroom.

In the car on the way to the theater, Mike turned an admiring glance on his glamorous date. "You look super. That Tom's an interesting conversationalist. He was telling me all about his job and the murder case he's on right now. Is there anything serious between you two? He seems very fond of you."

"I'm fond of Tom too. He's like my brother. We're very close friends. He says he's going to be my maid of honor when I get married."

"He'd look stunning in pink chiffon."

They both laughed.

"There's been a slight change in our plans for this evening, if it meets with your approval. My father is in town for a civil rights conference. He's invited us to join him for dinner in his hotel suite after the play. I don't get to see him very often so we always try to snatch time together whenever possible. He's a swell guy. You'll like him."

"Mike, I'd love to meet your father. He must be a fantastic person. I've read a lot about him."

"He did a great job with me after mom was killed in the car wreck. I was only ten when it happened.

"Oh, Mike."

"Yeah. He's a great guy!"

The haunting ballads and uproarious production numbers of the popular musical barely reached Linda. She applauded mechanically and laughed appropriately when Mike did, but her thoughts were on their later appointment.

I've got so much I want to ask him about. I must tell him how much I admire him. Wonder where he stands on the child-care bill. Some people say he wears a toupee. Now I'll find out for sure. Wish Tom could meet the Senator. He could ask some really probing questions. Hope I don't act like a tongue-tied fool. I hope he's as nice as Mike says. Sure hope his eyes are as blue as they were on the Life magazine cover.

Linda was shaken from her thoughts when the house lights came up and she became aware of Mike standing beside her offering his hand.

"Did you enjoy the play?"

"Oh yes, very much. Thank you."

Linda's anxiety began to build as they entered the palatial hotel lobby. She tried to control her trembling by studying the faces of the elegantly dressed people who stood around in clusters talking. Mike had the front desk clerk phone an announcement of their arrival to his father's suite. Mike's knock on the door of the top floor suite was answered by "Come in."

They entered to see the Senator seated at a desk strewn with papers. He held a telephone to his ear with one hand and a highball in the other. His wavy silver edged hair was ruffled and his glasses rested on his nose. His suit coat and tie were flung over the back of a chair and the rumpled white shirt he was wearing was open at the collar. Peering at them over his tilted spectacles, the Senator waved his glass towards the sofa, smiling an invitation for them to sit down. He ended his telephone call and rose to greet Linda and Mike. He embraced Mike in delight and repeated the bear hug for a surprised Linda. "Good to meet you," his voice boomed warmly. "Sit by me, Linda. My son's taste is improving every day."

Linda managed to squeeze out a quiet "How do you do?" before the Senator continued with his unabashed delight at having the opportunity to entertain them.

The chemistry between them was so strong that Linda was worried Mike would know she had fallen for his father before she even had time to sort out her emotions. She wanted the evening to end so she could analyze her feelings. Yet she hoped the evening would never end because she was enthralled by Senator Phil McPherson.

When Mike excused himself for a few minutes, Phil reached for Linda's hand. He looked unwaveringly into her eyes for a few seconds, and then quietly said the words she had been hoping to hear. "I'll talk to my son, and if Mike doesn't mind and you don't mind, then I'd like to call you."

"I'd like you to call, Phil."

"I will, Linda. I will."

On her flight the following evening, Linda and Betty were working the galley. As she set up dinner trays, Linda said, "Betty, I'm starving. Every morsel is tempting and even thoughts of the parsley have my tummy excited. I'm one of these people who eat when they're happy. Unfortunately, also when I'm sad."

"Perhaps there will be a tray left over."

"Dubs on it if there is."

Soon the meal service was completed. Linda started serving seconds on coffee. One male passenger shoved his untouched tray at her. "Take this away. I'm not hungry. Maybe later."

"Perhaps you might have either your salad or dessert, sir."

"I told you to take it away. I don't want it now. Do I have to spell it out for you! Move the tray!"

"Yes sir. Would you like some coffee?"

"I would like for you to leave me alone."

"Certainly sir." The man's rudeness did not dampen Linda's warm glowing feeling of new love. But his full tray of food did reach into her subconscious. With a single guilty thought of *Do I dare?*, she succumbed to temptation to eat the food, and was just finishing the tray of food in the galley when the stewardesses call button sounded.

Answering his summons, Linda was momentarily shaken. "I've changed my mind. I do want my dinner."

She looked at him then tried to smile. "I wish you hadn't said that, sir."

"Why? Did you eat my dinner?"

"You've flown before, haven't you?"

"Many times, now about my dinner?"

"Will you accept a meal authorization for the airport restaurant?" Linda was mentally composing a written explanation for her stewardess flight report."

"Hate those fool things. What is your name, young lady?"

"Linda Schuyler. I'm sorry about your tray."

"Give me the meal authorization."

Betty came up while Linda was completing her report and peeped over Linda's shoulder, then drew back and exclaimed, "You didn't."

Linda smirked. "Yes I did, Betty and I enjoyed every bite of it."

It was a week before Senator Phil McPherson called. "Hi, Linda. I had a few loose ends to tie up before I could make this call. When? When do we get together?"

"Hello, Senator. Since I'm the shy type, it'll be at least three hours before I can fly from Atlanta to Washington on Southaire, providing I leave my apartment right now."

"I'm delighted you're so bashful. I'll meet your plane."

Linda spent her three days off in Washington. She and Phil fed each other personal background material as if each was gathering and evaluating data. They were so compatible that exclamations of "me too" dotted their ongoing conversations.

Capricious love flitted through their hours together, night and day, as they enjoyed theater entertainment, a Senate banquet, walks in the parks, cab driver frustrations, a quiet sail, and candle light meals that lasted so long the candles melted into shimmering pools in their holders. And still they reached for each other and it was not enough.

"I'm glad you talked about us to Mike. I haven't seen him since our first date when I met you and knew I had to have you."

"That's the way it's got to be with me, Linda. No deceptions . . . never any deceptions. And by the way, if I don't tell you enough, I'm crazy about you."

Reluctantly, Linda returned to Atlanta for her next rotation flight to Los Angeles.

A newly married couple boarded with the groom wearing a ball and chain. A tuxedo clad groomsman carried the ball for the embarrassed new husband. Several of the formally attired members of the wedding party accompanied the newlyweds aboard. Linda was enjoying the merriment and waited until the last minute to shoo the non-flying group off the plane before takeoff. Holding out her hand, she asked the groomsman, "Where is the key and I'll unlock his shackles after you've deplaned."

"Key! Key? We have no key. He's got to get it off the best way he can."

"Ah c'mon! We're about ready for takeoff. I really do need the key."

The group started laughing at Linda's insistence. The groomsman turned his pocket out and said, "Honest! No key. Have a good trip. Bye, now."

Linda went to the cockpit. McLain Saranata was Captain. He whirled around. "What do youse want? Youse want to take the controls today?"

"No, Captain. I want to let you know we have a passenger in shackles."

"What?"

"Shackles! Ball and chain! A newlywed locked in a ball and chain, a very heavy ball." She grinned.

"Cripes! We's scheduled out on time for a change and youse come up and tell me this. Crimminey! Harold, go back and take a look. We can't go zooming around in the clouds with a ball rolling around in the cabin attached to some guy's . . .uh, where is it attached?"

She couldn't help grinning as she said, "His neck."

McLain exploded, "HIS NECK? The damn fool's got the thing around his neck?"

"He's not anymore pleased than you are."

Mac got up from his Captain's seat. "Never mind Harold. I'll take care of it."

The flight was delayed for half an hour while the newlywed was taken to a Southaire hanger and the neckpiece removed.

After the plane had been airborne for some five minutes, a four-year old asked Linda, "When are we going to get smaller?"

Linda squatted in the aisle beside her and asked, "What do you mean, get smaller?"

"You know," she replied with a giggle. "When airplanes go up in the sky they get littler and littler. When are we gonna get little?"

Linda smiled and replied, "To the people on the ground we're already small."

Soon the DC-9 reached the smooth suspended feeling above the clouds. The stew call button rang frantically. Linda hurried to a grandmotherly type woman sitting near a window. The woman jabbed her gnarled finger against the window pane. The flight was level and smooth.

Linda asked, "Yes, ma'am, what's wrong?"

The woman quickly reached up and grabbed Linda's sleeve. "Why have we stopped?"

Realizing the suspended feeling of the smooth ride, Linda calmed her. "We haven't stopped. It's just such a gorgeous day that Captain Saranata slowed down so you can enjoy looking out your window.

"Oh my. How nice of him." She settled against her seat. Linda fluffed a pillow, reclined the seat and inserted it behind the woman's gray hair.

"Call me if you need anything."

In Los Angeles operations, the crew was informed that they would have a cancer patient preboard on a stretcher. The woman passenger was heavily sedated with morphine. Her husband and son helped move her from the stretcher into a seat in the first class section. Linda reclined the seat, propped a pillow behind the woman's neck and covered her with a blanket. The weeping husband sat next to his dozing wife and the son sat across the aisle from his parents.

During the flight Linda visited with the son. He came to the buffet area for some orange juice. While they stood inside the partitioned area, he told Linda he was taking his parents home to Asheville, North Carolina. With tears brimming in his sorrowful brown eyes, he said. "Mom had wanted to make this trip to Riverside, California to see her sister. We almost waited too late. She had a bad spell while there and we had to stay an extra two weeks."

He drained his glass of juice and Linda refilled it. The flight was routine and Linda was glad she had time to listen.

"Pop also had a spell." His voice cracked and a tear trickled near his nose. "He had to have a couple of tests. The Doctor knew Mom's condition, so he told her Pop is okay, but, but . . ." he withdrew his handkerchief and blew his nose, "But, Pop isn't okay. The Doctor told me the tests were positive. Pop also has cancer. Doctor Smith said he only has six to eight months left. He doesn't know and I can't tell him." He started wiping his eyes with his handkerchief.

Linda put her arms about the grieving young man and tried to console him. "The Lord will guide you through this. If you can put your trust in God, it will be easier and somehow, with His guidance you'll be able to let your Dad know when the time is right. You'll find a reserve of extra strength when you have to tell him he also has cancer. The doctor in California must have known you could handle this. And somehow, with God's help, you'll be able to carry this full load. Also, try to think of your Mom passing into a place where she won't need morphine for pain because there will be no more pain. And help your Dad to understand."

"Thank you. I feel better just being able to talk to somebody. So far, I'm the only one that knows. You're very kind to listen and it's a surprise to find out you're such a Christian. I never thought about an airline stewardess being religious. It's a surprise. A real surprise."

"It shouldn't be. Christians can be everywhere, even in the galley."

Chapter 17—Go Brunhilde, Go!

The rain fell in gray sheets over the airplane and made plumes of glistening spray behind the wheels as it taxied toward the bright lights of the terminal.

Linda bid a farewell to her passengers and helped the ill family get situated in the ambulance that waited at the foot of the ramp. By the time she had gathered her belongings and began descending the ramp steps, the rain had nearly stopped. A breeze threw a chilly spray of rain in Linda's face as she ran across the tarmac, dodging pools of shimmering water reflecting lights from the airport on the asphalt. She was a woman with a mission. After her depressing flight she wanted one thing . . . the warm, secure presence of Senator Phil McPherson. She was determined to spend as much time with him as she could arrange.

Crew scheduling was empty when Linda went in. A cigarette smoldering in an overflowing astray proved that someone was around somewhere. Linda didn't care. She hadn't come here to visit. Taking pad and pen from her pocketbook, Linda looked up the schedule assignments for the next month on flights to Washington, D.C. She jotted down the names of the stewardesses assigned to the DCA rotation and vowed to call them and arrange as many swaps as she could. She was to the point where she would even swap her car Brunhilde for a flight to Washington. Someone came up to the counter beside her. Linda turned and saw another stewardess whose red hair and turned up nose were vaguely familiar.

"Jackie Gilcrest?" she asked hopefully. This was one of the names on the DCA rotation list.

"Yeah, you're Linda something-or-other. I'm sorry, I can't remember."

"Schuyler, but don't worry about it. You look bushed."

"I am. I bailed out my roommate and took her Detroit flight because she was not feeling well and this awful weather had us delayed for hours. I'll just have time to get home and rest a bit before I have to be back here for the eye opener to Washington."

She leaned tiredly against the counter. She smiled at Linda and teased, "I'll give you a nickel if you take my Washington flight."

"I'll even give you a quarter if you let me have it," Linda explained to a surprised Jackie.

As soon as she got home, Linda called Phil. "I'll be there at 0900," she told him. "I fly back out at 0600. We don't have to do anything special. I just need to be with you. I'm so lonesome."

"Linda, dear, I have to be on the floor all day tomorrow, there's an important bill coming up. I'll send a car to meet you and bring you to the Senate office. All I can offer you is a seat in the gallery and lunch. I'm sorry and disappointed that we can't be together—really together—but I can look at you and know you are near. And we will have a long lunch."

"Oh Phil, don't give it another thought. That will be enough. Besides, I'm dying to see you in action."

Linda couldn't sleep. She spent the night trying on clothes to find the perfect Senate gallery outfit, washing and rolling her hair, and giving herself a manicure.

She was at the airport an hour earlier than she needed to be the next morning. Her sleepy passengers spent the flight being catered to by an unusually chipper stewardess. Linda smiled brightly from takeoff, through coffee and roll service, to hearty goodbyes at the exit door. After changing into the outfit she had brought, Linda met Phil's driver at the South-aire desk. She soon found herself in the corridor of Senate Office Building at the door to Senator McPherson's office.

While she was trying to decide whether to knock or walk in, Phil came striding down the hall followed by an aide. She was swept up into his embrace, kissed firmly and led into the office. Phil introduced Linda to his staff, handed her a cup of coffee and rushed off after instructing a secretary to take Linda to the gallery in thirty minutes for the opening of the Senate. Kathy, the secretary, took Linda on a scenic route to the Senate chambers. Linda was as impressed as a schoolgirl with the overwhelming atmosphere of history that filled the Capital.

She watched with pride as Phil presented an impassioned speech in favor of the bill coming up, and she cheered silently when the majority of the Senate voted their agreement with Phil. Snatching whatever time they could for coffee breaks and a nice long lunch, Linda and Phil were nevertheless able to share a deep, satisfying time, communicating with their eyes, words and caressing hands.

After a whirlwind of happiness, Linda too soon found herself at the airport in time to be a stewardess for her flight home. She was confused about the new found love and extremely tired, but was content with the day. *I'm making this trip as often as I can arrange it,* she vowed to herself as she watched the first passenger come up the stairs."

On the return flight from Washington, movie star Robert Mitchum demanded a highball when he boarded. Linda smiled and replied, "Do you think you can wait until we're airborne, Mr. Mitchum?"

Flashing a famous grin he told her he would only wait if she would be the one to bring it to him. Weary of flirtatious men, she replied sarcastically, "Oh, it would be my pleasure, sir."

Immersed in flight duties, it was awhile before Linda got around to delivering drink orders. Mitchum was indignant at the delay, but proffered forgiveness if she would have dinner with him.

"You're very kind to ask me, but it's been a long day, and all I can think about is collapsing at home as soon as possible . . . alone." Turning away abruptly from Linda, he grabbed the hand of another passing stewardess and requested that she fix him another drink.

Before landing in Atlanta, a male passenger started walking toward the lavatories. Suddenly his eyes rolled back and he keeled forward, striking his head on an arm rest as he fell. Linda and a co-helper rushed to him. He was unconscious. The other stewardess grabbed the medical kit and Linda broke an ammonia ampoule and waved it under his nose. He groaned but did not regain consciousness. A spot of blood oozed from the cut on his chin where he had hit the arm rest. Using an antiseptic swab from her med-kit, Linda wiped the cut while the other stewardess got the portable oxygen bottle. Together they cautioned everyone in the vicinity to not smoke near the oxygen, and put the face mask on the inert man.

When he was conscious, he had no earthly idea of what had happened to him and could offer no explanation. He deplaned with other passengers and assured the stewardesses he felt fine. He promised them he would go to his physician early the next morning for a complete physical.

Linda trudged wearily to the Southaire employee parking lot and started talking to the car she called Brunhilde. "Damn it, you'd better start tonight and get me home without any backtalk, or your days with me are numbered." The car must have heard her. She got home without incident.

Linda's friend Tom woke her about mid-morning with a phone call, and she realized how exhausted she must be to sleep that late.

"Hi ya, Linda, got a hot item, and I quote . . . What young stewardess with a Southern based airline has been seen in the company of an attractive, eligible Senator from the Midwest?"

"Oh no!" Linda responded in distress. "Where are you reading that? Phil doesn't like that kind of publicity."

"Joke, Linda, just a joke. I made it up. I didn't read it."

"Damn it, Tom, you scared me."

"I'm sorry, good buddy. I thought you'd appreciate the humor. You must be more hung up on that guy than I realized." He cut off her sputtering with a question. "When do I get to meet the Senator, anyway? I want to make sure this guy's good enough for you."

"Just as soon as we can arrange it, he wants to meet you too. I know you'll like each other."

"Let's talk about him some more over dinner tonight."

"I accept your invitation," Linda replied.

"Great! I'll bring the beer. Remember, I like my roast beef rare."

"You are truly one of the last of the big spenders, Tom Bensen," Linda said to the dial tone.

The next day Linda was spending an evening with her supervisor friend, Sue. After a sandwich, they decided to go to a near-by ice cream parlor for a super banana split treat. On the drive in the behaving Brunhilde, Linda joked, "Ya know, Sue, when I'm happy, my appetite controls me and boy am I happy. So happy in fact that I might eat two splits."

She kept glancing in the rear view mirror and her lilting tone changed. "Sue, I don't mean to be an alarmist, but I believe we're being followed."

Sue half shifted and watched the trailing car as Linda maneuvered Brunhilde through a couple of out-of-the-way blocks to verify her suspicions. Sue nodded. "What the hell? Linda, I don't like this at all. We sure are being followed. Let's go on to the ice cream parlor. There'll be people there and we can get help."

Watching the headlights of the trailing vehicle, Linda commented, "Ya know, Sue, things like this really worry me. There are so many kooks loose nowadays. Can you see the driver at all?"

"Not really, the headlights are too bright."

Linda parallel parked her shabby little Volkswagen as close as she could to the entrance of the crowded ice cream parlor. Still, there was a good fifty yard walk between them and the door.

They had lost sight of the car that had been following them. Looking around for any unusual characters, Linda and Sue jumped from Brunhilde and headed toward the restaurant at a brisk walk.

"I'm going to kill you." A hysterical voice shrieked behind them, freezing Linda and Sue where they stood. Linda slowly turned to see a tall, slim woman with a carefully coiffure bouffant hairdo clutching a pocketbook and standing against a darkened store window.

Sue boldly turned around and said, "You're making a mistake! Why would you want to kill us?"

The woman's high pitched voice reached out from the shadows. "I don't want to kill you. I'm going to kill her, Miss La-di-dah Linda Schuyler.

Linda was filled with anger and fear. "I never did anything to you. I don't even know you."

"You call stealing my husband nothing? You're just a cheap tramp and I'm not going to let you live."

"Calm down," Linda said as the approached the woman slowly. "I don't even know your husband."

"Don't come any closer." Her hand reached into her pocketbook as she stepped out into the pool of light from a street lamp. "I have a gun. Don't lie to me, tramp. I know you're having an affair with my husband. I saw you two last week. Frank was holding your arm and you were laughing and talking together so that anyone would know. You have no shame."

"Frank? Frank Lancaster?" Linda was befuddled.

"Don't pretend you don't know who I mean. I'm Betty Lancaster."

Linda was astonished. "Frank's one of the pilots on my rotation!" She turned pleadingly toward Sue. "Sure I know him and we're friends, but I've never seen him outside of working hours."

"LIAR!" she screamed. Then Betty Lancaster stepped between Sue and Linda and turned toward Linda. "I'm going to keep you from breaking up any other marriages." She pointed a small gleaming gun that looked like a toy toward Linda's head.

A group of people stood watching in the door of the ice cream parlor. They were talking excitedly among themselves but no one made a move to help. Mrs. Lancaster's scream, "You tramp!" was cut off in a gurgle as Sue's left arm came around her throat and her right hand grabbed the woman's wrist, pointing the gun toward the pavement.

"I can't hold you like this forever. You can still shoot Linda, but you will also have to shoot me and all those people over there. We know who you are. What will you gain shooting Linda? Frank won't want to stay married to a murderess. He'll find somebody else. Let me have the gun and you get yourself out of here and I won't call the police."

Betty Lancaster dropped the gun. Obviously fighting for self control she avoided their angry eyes as she fled back to her Cadillac.

Linda smiled weakly at Sue and said, "What can I say? Thank you isn't enough."

Sue took her hand and replied, "You order two super-dooper banana splits while I call Frank."

In a short time Sue returned from the pay phone booth and sat down heavily in the frail ice cream parlor chair across from the waiting Linda.

"What was his reaction when you called?"

"Naturally he was upset and you'll be getting an apology from him."

Linda angrily shoved the banana split forward in front of her and leaned on folded arms. "I don't want an apology! I want someone to care for that poor, misguided woman. Can you imagine the distress she must experience every time he goes on a flight? Oh, Lord, Sue, if people would only take the time to comfort each other. If only they would share, care and love. That's what life is really all about. We have such a loving Savoir. If only people would practice what we learn in Church, so much heartache could be prevented. It makes me boil. Instead of Frank Lancaster calling me to apologize for his wife, he should take her in his arms and they should get down on their knees and thank the Lord for you stopping her from shooting me."

She lowered her eyes and slid her ice cream back in front of her. "I'm sorry, Sue, but I do get carried away sometimes.

Ah well, this will cool me down." She scooped a large bite of the melting vanilla cream into her mouth.

Two days later during a flight from Savannah, a passenger who was traveling with her 18-month old son developed severe pains in her arms and chest and had difficulty breathing. Linda administered oxygen while another stewardess held the frightened child. When the flight landed in Atlanta, Linda volunteered to accompany the woman in the ambulance to Grady Hospital to help care for the little son. An Airline Agent stopped her.

"You don't have to help. They'll take care of that kid someway. Black people always manage to get cared for."

Linda took a deep, angry breath. "Look, friend, I volunteered to help simply because it is a human being who needs help. She could be purple with antennas sticking out her head and I'd still help. That baby doesn't know one color from another and I'd hate to be the one to let him know the difference tonight when his Mother might die."

"You bleeding heart liberals are all alike."

Linda climbed into the back of the ambulance. She knew if she answered the Southaire co-worker there would be a scene.

At Grady, the woman was placed in Intensive Care and her husband notified in Columbus, Ohio. He decided to wait until morning before making travel plans. If his wife was able to continue her trip, he wanted her put on a plane to Columbus. Linda talked long distance with him, asked the son's name and got his permission to take the 18-month old youngster home with her. Linda was more than ready for the call from Ricky's mother in a couple of hours telling her she would be able to be released the next day and would fly on to Columbus.

Linda had spent a frenzied evening running one step ahead of the active bright-eyed boy trying to childproof her cluttered apartment. His energy had been as unceasing as his charm. Linda alternated between wanting a child of her own and swearing off parenthood forever.

After a brief night's sleep, she took Ricky to the airport to be reunited with his mother. She handed Ricky to his mother in the takeoff waiting area. He wrapped his pudgy brown arms around Linda's neck and gave her graham cracker crumb kiss. To a ruddy faced man who sat staring in shock at the display of affection, Linda grinned and said, "He's my grandson" before she walked off.

On her next night coach to New York, Linda was making a seat belt check prior to takeoff. Phil was meeting her in New York, so she was thoughtfully distracted from her routine duties aboard and was not quick in grasping the situation when she encountered a coach passenger sitting in his underwear. Linda was two seats beyond when realization hit her. She quickly backed up. She tapped the slight middle-aged man on the shoulder and asked, "Where are your pants?"

He grinned. "Thank you."

Linda gestured to his hairy legs. "Your trousers . . . your clothes! Where are your pants?"

He made a bow toward her. "Thank you. Thank you."

The plane was shrieking down the runway. Momentarily stymied, Linda rushed to her seat and buckled in just before the powerful plane soared skyward.

Pondering the situation of the underwear clad gentleman, Linda thought, *well, obviously he doesn't understand a word I'm saying. Surely he wore pants on board. Otherwise, I believe one of us would have noticed.* After the seatbelt light was extinguished, she approached the man again.

"Parlez-vous Français?" she inquired with her limited French vocabulary.

He smiled questioningly and said, "Thank you."

She shrugged and said aloud, "Well, it isn't French." She grabbed another stewardess as she walked by.

"Do you know any languages, Spanish, Arabic, Japanese, anything? Evidentially, this man doesn't speak English."

Startled the girl replied, "I can say hello in Dutch."

"Try it."

The other stewardess attempt met with the same response, "Thank you."

The stewardess immediately turned to Linda, arms up in the air, wide apart. "Where are his pants? He didn't board like that, did he?"

"That's what I'm trying to find out."

Throughout the flight Linda asked various people to try out a second language with the man. Each try was answered with a heavily accented, "Thank you."

At the end of the flight, he went to the closet and carefully removed his sharply creased pants and immaculate coat. After dressing in the closet area, he reached into his flight bag, withdrew a bottle of cologne and liberally applied it to this face and neck. Departing in a cloud of lilac fragrance, the dapper little man turned to the amazed flight attendants, bowed and said "Thank you."

Chapter 18—Keep Circling, the Snake is still Missing

Southaire Corporation merged with Westway Transcontinental Service. This growth added new cities of Seattle, Washington, Portland, Oregon, Boise, Idaho and Butte, Montana to the route, launching a 36 million dollar jet expansion program. With the purchase of four additional Convair 880s and four DC-8s in the mid-Sixties, Southaire purchased IBM Sabre, a computer-based electronic airline reservation system.

The death of A. F. Williams, Founder and President of Southaire was mourned throughout the nation. McLain Saranata, pilot and long-time friend, was interviewed by TV News before boarding a flight.

"Da boss was the most human person in the world. His passing into da great blue beyond is a sad event. A. F. was a friend to everyone who ever worked for him, no matter what job. Me and him shared so many things in da early days that I can't even count up our adventures. To be a friend wid A. F. was like knowin' there was always fresh bread in da cubbord when yer kids was hungry. It's like, like, it was, uh, friendship with A. F. was like security. I can't say no more."

His voice cracked with emotion. "He is a great man, always has been and always will be, no matter dat he is no longer wid us. I'm proud to have been his friend."

McLain took off his uniform cap and bowed his head. The TV camera swept the background where multiple jet airplanes, all bearing the Southaire ensign, were found. The shot faded with an insert shot of a DC-2 aircraft.

More changes were made. In the late sixties, stewardess uniforms for the jet age were designed by La Rue, chief designer for a large movie studio. Shoulder length hair was allowed on flight attendants, and passengers were permitted to carry on articles which could be placed under their seats.

On an 880, Los Angeles, Dallas, New Orleans, Birmingham, Atlanta run, several teenagers boarded in Dallas carrying cartons, plants and creative paraphernalia bound for a Science Fair in Atlanta. The flight was due in Atlanta at 0200. Linda was patrolling the happy passengers, many slumbering in the semi-dark cabin. As she reached the forward section, one of the teenagers came rushing to her from the coach section.

"Amy has lost her snake. It's gotten loose."

"What?"

"Amy's snake . . . her science project. She had it in a box under her seat. It's gone!"

"Let's go! Is it poisonous?"

"I dunno! Ask Amy!"

They raced toward the rear of the cabin. Several kids were on their hands and knees crawling between seats. Linda understood the potential panic among her sleeping passengers. If she were to suddenly jar them awake with the announcement 'A snake is loose'.

Mustering as much calm as possible and still trying to be aware of where she was placing her own thin soled shoes, Linda softly asked, "Which one's Amy?"

"I am," the flushed, spectacled girl answered from the floor between rows of seats.

"Is it poisonous?"

"No ma'am. It's harmless and probably scared nearly to death."

"We'll find it. We'd better find it." She crossed her fingers. "Keep searching. I'll be back."

She moved gingerly to the buffet and lifted the intercom, flicked the cockpit switch and asked, "How much longer to Birmingham?"

"'Bout 20 more minutes until I turn on the belt sign? Why? Got a problem?"

"Sort of. There's a snake loose."

"Lady, you got a problem!"

"Thanks. Come help look."

"No way! I'm scared of snakes!"

After conferring with the other stewardesses, she decided they simply had to turn on the overhead lights and tell the passengers what was going on. They agreed this was the best approach, rather than have a passenger discover the snake and maybe have a heart attack, or panic and open an exit door in flight. While the public announcement was being made, the other stewardesses began a slow transfer of scared, sleepy, mumbling people from coach seats up into the first class section into a small space not designed to hold 150 nervous passengers.

After the coach was emptied, the seat belt sign came on. Linda rushed past the packed crowd into the cockpit. "We can't land right now. Call the Tower and get permission to circle. We've got all the passengers crowded into the front section. We're looking for that damn snake."

"Okay, boss lady. We'll circle. But hurry. One of these days I'm gonna put on a stew uniform and just see how you can screw up a routine flight so badly."

"I'll gladly change uniforms with you right now." Her hand reached for the top button of her red knit tunic.

He pointed toward the cockpit door and ordered, "Go!"

The search was on. Items were moved from beneath seats, attaché cases and handbags were opened, and even overhead racks were searched. The 880 stayed in a holding pattern while the clock played havoc with airline scheduled timetables. After what seemed like an interminable search, the vagabond science fair exhibit was found curled beneath a seat cushion and partially wrapped around the stabilizer bar of the seat.

Amy and a friend began tugging, trying to free the snake. He was wound tightly and too petrified to let go. Amy sat in the seat next to her pet. The passengers were returned to coach and the flight touched down in Birmingham 45 minutes late.

When an agent boarded, the problem of the coiled snake was explained. He went for a mechanic, while the plane was evacuated. It took several minutes of tugging hard by the

Agent and mechanic. Watching both them and Amy's face, Linda was afraid the men would pull the teenagers pet apart, but finally they managed to free the snake. Soon it was secure in a container in Amy's lap. Passengers were re-boarded and the flight continued on to Atlanta with some very wide awake passengers for four a.m. in the morning.

Linda collapsed in her apartment and did nothing constructive for two days. On the third morning, with great apprehension, she readied herself for her trip to Las Vegas. It was as miserable as she had anticipated. Passengers were air sick, head cold sick, demanding, complaining. And there was a mechanical delay of five hours in which the stewardesses had to pacify the unhappy passengers.

On the capacity loaded, busy return flight between Las Vegas and Dallas, one of the stewardesses had an attack of probable appendicitis. Linda and the other stewardess, Cathy, doubled up the work load. The ailing girl was strapped into a jump seat with an ice pack on her abdomen and a burp bag in her hand.

A tall, rather average looking businessman in a pin stripe serge suit offered to help the harried stewardesses. He declared he knew how to set up trays in the buffet. With the airliner cruising at a record speed, the attendants were grateful for any help. The passenger washed his hands, removed his suit jacket, rolled up his sleeves and went to work. He skillfully pulled the skeleton trays from the storage rack, removed hot entrées from warmer ovens, and arranged them with salad, dessert, bread and beverage, deftly handing them to the stewardesses to be delivered to the waiting passengers. While he controlled the buffet areas, the stewardesses were free to efficiently go about their other cabin duties and attend to the needs of their sick friend.

In Dallas the ill stewardess was rushed onto a waiting ambulance. The helpful man deplaned, brushing aside the girl's grateful thanks for his help in the meal service.

Later in the evening, after termination of the flight in Atlanta, and all passengers had deplaned, the girls were skimming the cabin in last minute duties.

Linda remarked, "Tomorrow is Sue's birthday. I'm gonna stop by the gift shop and get her a silly present and stick it on her desk in the stewardess office so she'll find it in the morning. If you don't mind waiting, I'll drop you off at your apartment on the way home."

As she and Linda retrieved their purses from the buffet, Cathy replied, "Oh thanks, that'd be great."

Inside the terminal gift boutique, Linda picked out a paperback book on 'How to Conquer Your Fear of Flying' and asked to have it gift-wrapped. Pulling her wallet out, she exclaimed, "What the hell? I had more than $20.00. It's gone!" She dug in her purse. "My checkbook is gone too."

Cathy leaned toward her friend to peer inside the purse. "You haven't left your purse some where unattended, have you? Your checkbook could be in your overnight case. Maybe your money too."

"No. I cashed a check at the hotel just before we started this trip in Vegas. I definitely had the money and checkbook right here in my purse and the only time it wasn't on my shoulder was when it was in the buffet during the flight. Well, damn. Now I gotta call the bank to block my account and get new checks. Guess I'll get Sue something tomorrow."

Cathy reached for her billfold and said, "Here, I've got some money. I'll pay for this and you can repay me later." She pulled out her wallet. "Good gosh, my money's gone too! Linda we've been robbed! Some dirty bum has taken our dough. Who would rob us? Surely not a Southaire employee or passenger. Besides our purses were kept in the buffet during . . ."

They looked at each other. Cathy snapped her fingers . . . "Old Helpful Harry! The guy with the meal service . . .!"

Linda wrinkled her brow and said, "Surely . . . surely not . . . he wouldn't, would he? Where'd he get off?"

"Here? No! Dallas, I think! Did you get his name?"

"No. never thought about it." Linda shrugged. "Guess we're just out of luck."

"Not luck . . . moola! Well, that's the way it goes."

"Yeah. Guess I'll scribble Happy Birthday on a tissue with my lipstick and put it on Sue's desk," Cathy exclaimed with vengeance. "Wherever he is, I hope he gets mugged before he can spend our money."

They drove silently home, each with thoughts of how lousy people can be at times.

"Boy, we sure were taken for a couple of suckers," Linda exclaimed to Tom over pizza and beer. She had just brought him up to date on her latest adventure in the sky when the doorbell rang. Linda, barefooted and in jeans, opened the door to a uniformed delivery man holding two huge white boxes.

"Miss Schuyler?" he questioned uncertainly as he eyed her casual appearance.

"Yes."

"These are for you, with the compliments of a friend," the delivery man said as he handed one box to Linda and one to Tom who was by now standing behind her.

"What on earth?" Linda said as she removed the lid of her box. "Good grief. Yellow roses, jillions of yellow roses. What's in that box, Tom?"

He opened it and looked inside. "More yellow roses. You planning to redecorate in yellow or something, Linda? There must be six dozen here."

"Don't just stand there holding them, look for a card. They have to be from Phil but . . . damn . . . damn . . . I don't know what possessed him to buy this many roses."

Linda was sucking her finger after an unsuccessful search through sharp thorns for a card when the doorbell rang again.

"Get that for me please. If it's more roses tell the man he's got the wrong house," Linda told Tom as she carried an armful of the golden blooms into the kitchen in search of a vase, or rather several vases.

"Linda, come sign for a telegram," Tom called.

"Good grief. What now? I hate telegrams, they always bring bad news." Linda sat with the unopened yellow envelope in her lap.

"Open it ninny." Tom said in exasperation.

"Here!" She thrust it at him. "You read it to me. I don't think I can make my eyes focus. I just keep seeing hundreds of yellow roses."

Tom pulled out the telegram and unfolded it slowly.

"Oh, hurry up!"

"I thought you didn't like telegrams," he teased.

"Darling," he read in his most romantic Charles Boyer imitation. "I hope you like the flowers. Yellow is the color of sunshine and therefore the color for you."

Linda snatched at the telegram. "Okay, I can read the rest for myself. Give it to me."

Tom held it over his head and far beyond Linda's reach. "I always finish what I start. Either I read it or no one will. Take your choice."

"All right, dammit, you win. But you're coming mighty close to making me mad."

"Aw shucks, ma'am, you're so pretty when you're mad."

"Shut up and read!"

"I love you and I need you," the telegram continued. "I hope you feel the same. I will be calling you tonight around nine. Please be home. All my love, Phil."

Tom finally handed her the telegram. "I'd say, just an off-hand guess, mind you, that the guy's hung up on you. Hope he's not going to be disappointed."

"Tom, you know I love him. I've never felt this way about anyone before. He is everything I ever wanted in a man."

"You sure know how to hurt a guy," Tom moaned in mock rejection. Casually picking up his beer, he glanced at his watch and remarked, "By the way, it's one minute to nine. Wanna bet he forgets your phone number?"

Tom was saved from a savage beating with a throw pillow by the shrill ring of the telephone. As Linda eagerly scooped up the receiver, Tom took the dishes to the kitchen to give her some measure of privacy.

"Hello? Phil?"

"Hello, darling. How are you?"

"Up to my . . . um . . . knees in yellow roses but fine otherwise. You're crazy, you know it?"

"Yeah, crazy in love. Do you realize that the whole country is suffering because we're apart?"

"I'm suffering, and you are too, but the whole country? Come on."

"The best Senator in Washington is running around like a love sick schoolboy. Therefore, he's not getting anything done. Therefore the whole country is suffering."

"That's what I've always loved about you . . . your humility."

"Seriously, Linda. I'm set to go on a fact finding trip to Europe for a month and I want you with me . . . as my wife, of course. Can you get ready to come to Washington and marry me before this weekend? I know it means you won't be able to have a big, fancy wedding . . ."

"Phil, I'll be there, you know I will and I'll bring my fancy wedding with me . . . the world's tallest maid of honor! Tom."

"That's wonderful, Linda. I love you. I don't think I can wait. Don't you have a flight to Washington tomorrow?"

"Yes, but it's a turn-around."

"Well, only take this part up here and don't plan to turn-around. Notify the airline that you're making a one way trip."

"That soon, huh? Just like that?"

"That's it, babe. No sense in fooling around. I'm a man of action. We'll go right from the airport for blood tests. I'll take care of the paperwork and cut some red tape and we'll be married before you could even complete the turn-around portion of your trip."

"Phil, is this the way our life together is going to be?"

"I hope so. Don't you?"

With a smile in her voice she replied emphatically. "Uh huh, I sure do. I adore you."

"I adore you too, Mrs. Senator."

"What about Mike? I just thought about Mike, Phil. Shouldn't he be told or be at the wedding or something since he is your only son and . . ."

"I'll get Mike up here. But I had to know if you'd come first before I told Mike."

"You knew I would."

"Linda, I almost knew you would. I don't take you that much for granted."

"Ya better not ever."

"I won't. I just want to take you."

They talked for fifteen minutes more before reluctantly hanging up. She showed Tom out the door and sent him home to pack. Then Linda spent the rest of that night choosing the right clothes to put in the one suitcase Phil had told her to bring. He said he'd buy her anything else she needed on the trip. She wrote a hurried letter of resignation to Southaire and notes of marriage announcement to some of her close friends. Between calls to her parents and relatives, Linda answered frantic telephone calls from Tom.

First, he wanted to tell her he had arranged to get the time off from work. Then he called back to ask her where and when to meet her for the flight. Next he called to ask what a male maid of honor wears. He pestered Linda with questions until she ordered him not to speak to her again until they were on their way to Washington the next day.

Before boarding passengers for her last flight as a Southaire stewardess, Linda was greeted by an agent.

"Got you a super-dooper celebrity. We're gonna board him early to avoid a fan jam in the waiting room. He's in the VIP lounge now."

"Bet I know who it is. It's William Holden. He's making a movie in Washington and has been on a lot of Southaire flights lately. Several of the girls have been talking about how smooth he is."

Realizing in a few hours she would be a married woman, an impish bit of last minute freedom caused her to add with an exaggerated leer, "You can board him right now and keep the rest of the passengers for about 30 minutes."

The agent grinned and waved as he departed to fetch the celebrity from Southaire's courtesy room.

In a few minutes Linda was startled to hear deep, heavy barking. The agent yelled, "Here's your guest of honor, Rin Tin Tin. He's telling you hello. Mister Tin, this is your senior stewardess, Miss Linda Schuyler." The agent was really enjoying the joke. The dog sat down and put out a paw. Being a good sport, Linda bent over and shook the forepaw of her early boarding VIP.

Linda was counting on a few undisturbed minutes during takeoff to think about her status as the future Mrs. McPherson, but the DC-9 had barely taken off for Washington when the stewardess call button sounded frantically. Linda unbuckled her seat belt and hurried to the area. An elderly gentleman leaned across a semi-conscious woman and quickly explained, "There's something wrong with this lady. Before takeoff she started perspiring. Then, during takeoff, she had difficulty speaking. Now she says she's dizzy."

Linda felt the woman's brow. It was warm and damp. She asked, "Can you tell me what's wrong, ma'am?" The woman bobbed her head from side to side but her words were incoherent and barely audible. They were punctuated with groans.

Linda asked the man, "Are you traveling together? Do you know what's wrong?"

With a wrinkled, worried expression, he answered, "I never saw her before. Sorry. I can't help."

Linda went for an ampoule of smelling salts and a wet cloth. She applied both, but neither had much effect on the woman. In desperation, Linda grabbed the woman's pocketbook and dumped it upside down in her lap. As soon as she saw the bottle of insulin and the hypodermic syringe, Linda realized the woman was a diabetic. She took the woman by the shoulders and asked loudly, "Do you need an injection? Is that the problem?"

The woman shook her head violently and a few faint words escaped her lips, "Too much already, didn't eat . . ."

Linda rushed to the buffet, prepared a glass of orange juice with extra sugar dumped in, then hurried back to her critical passenger. She and the elderly man kept pouring the sweet, syrupy liquid into the lady until she regained full consciousness.

The flight was nearly over before Linda had a chance to speak to Tom. When she approached his seat, she saw that he was sleeping soundly. In retribution for the nuisance he had made of himself the previous night, Linda picked up a pillow and hit him soundly on the head saying, "Wake up, sir, we're almost to Washington."

The other passengers stared in shock as Linda strolled calmly on checking seatbelts, while Tom muttered ornery threats at her back.

As Linda and Tom walked across the pavement towards Phil McPherson and his grinning son, Linda squeezed Tom's arm affectionately.

"Just think, today is my wedding day. I've already saved the life of a woman, shook hands with a famous dog, and it's not even noon."

The Seventies

Are you ready for a rewarding career?

Airline Flight Attendants have wanderlust. They enjoy traveling to places they have never been. They are energetic, forward thinking, educated, attractive "people pleasers." Flight Attendants must be versatile, quick thinking, and willing to accept responsibility for many passengers. Southaire Flight Attendants lost the "Stewardess" tag when men were also considered for this position.

Benefits

Flexibility of schedules, teamwork in working a rotation, interesting locations of flights, meeting passengers in all walks of life, good salaries, 85 hours a month on duty and ample time off.

Can you qualify?

If you are the person who has these qualities, there may be a rewarding career for you.

- ✦ Are you single? Flight Attendants may marry and retain their job.
- ✦ Do you enjoy traveling, the flexibility of flight scheduling?
- ✦ Do you relate well to people, to crowds?
- ✦ What is your attitude in an emergency?
- ✦ Are you dependable and understanding?
- ✦ Do you have any health problems?
- ✦ Do you have a high moral character?
- ✦ Do you have two years of college or equivalent business work?
- ✦ Are you 21 or older?

+ Have you good vision or wear contact lens successfully?
+ Do you speak a foreign language?
+ Are you versatile in your base living location?

If you meet our qualifications, we will arrange a personal interview with you.

Chapter 19—Your Friendliest Stowaway, Ever!

"I'll be damned if I'll wear ridiculous hot pants on an airplane," Stephanie exclaimed as she turned from reading the bulletin board in Southaire's flight attendant lounge. "My job is to provide for customer's . . . uh . . . passenger's safety and comfort. Not to parade around showing off my legs, feeding the fantasies of sexist old men."

Another flight attendant, at least 5 inches shorter than the willowy Stephanie chimed in with her opinion. "I don't know what you're grousing about. With your legs, you'd keep 'em tongue-tied. I'm the one who should worry." She looked ruefully at her sturdy calves and ankles showing below her skirt hemline.

"That's not the point!" Stephanie replied angrily. "I'm not going to let the airline turn me into a centerfold. They have no right to make us wear silly little outfits just to boost ticket sales. We deserve respect as women, not dress up dolls. And I, for one, will not stand for this!"

Stephanie warmed up to her subject as she continued lecturing the handful of flight attendants that sat around the lounge. "We have to demand respect. Women have put up with this kind of nonsense for too long. I'll draw up a petition that we can all sign, refusing to wear hot pants just because Southaire want us to."

A slim, smiling woman in a Southaire uniform entered the room. Her sleek coiffure hid a few gray strands and laugh lines played around the corners of her eyes and mouth.

"What are you on your soap box about this time, Steph?"

"Just read that notice about hot pants over there," she said as she waved towards the bulletin board. The older woman stood and read the directive with great concentration. When she had finished, she turned to her friend who awaited her cry of outrage.

"I don't suppose you noticed where it said hot pants would be strictly optional. No one is going to have to wear them."

"Where does it say that?"

"Right here in the bottom paragraph."

After verification, Stephanie turned once again from the bulletin board and gave Doris a lop-sided grin. "Okay, so it isn't mandatory. But hell . . . they shouldn't have thought of it in the first place."

With a shrug, and as a final outlet for her steam, she remarked, "Oh well, there'll be other things to fight." She winked at her shorter colleague. "How are you, Doris? What's with the family? Any mumps, measles, syphilis, or . . ." In the Seventies, flight attendants were allowed to be married.

"Stephanie! You're a hopeless case. The kids are fine, the hubby is fine. I'm fine."

The two opposites stood chatting off center of the flight attendant area before starting pre-boarding activities.

Stephanie Irene Saranata was tall, leggy and slim, with close-cropped, no-nonsense black hair, and brown, sparkling eyes. Wearing little or no make-up, and with lush, enviable eyelashes, Stephanie was a second generation airline person. Her mother, Pauline O'Shannon had been among the historically first stewardess class. Her father, Captain McLain Saranata, had been (behind his back) affectionately called Monster Mac by all who flew with him because of his direct way of saying exactly what was on his mind. Stephanie was a compelling mixture of her flamboyant parents . . . a combination of her mother's beauty and intellect, and her father's direct bluntness and strength.

Doris Spencer Russell was a re-hire, the antithesis of Stephanie. Small, fair, gentle, and passive, she was a phenomenon of the Seventies . . . a former stewardess who had left to get married, returning to continue the job she loves, juggling career and motherhood to reap the benefits of additional income.

Doris and Stephanie worked side by side in routine duties. They busied themselves with signing the crew check-in sheet, checking the television screen for flight number, gate number, estimated time of arrival for their through flight arrival, scheduled time of departure, and seeing whether theirs was an equipment change, delay or change in catering. They checked the bulletin board, flight schedules for future trips, their mailboxes, and then answered company mail. They checked personal equipment of liquor kit keys, their small flashlights and liquor money to give passengers change when they purchased a drink. After glancing at the clock, they obtained the necessary flight pay forms and made a last minute personal appearance check in front of the mirrored wall.

Satisfied they were Southaire's finest, Steph asked, "Ready, pardner?"

Boarding the DC-9 bound for New York, the flight attendants went to their assigned pre-flight duties. Stephanie was working senior in first class, while Doris was working senior stewardess in tourist, with May Phillips serving as her junior helper. May was young and fairly inexperienced, and she stood in awe of her senior flight attendant who was old enough to be her mother.

Stephanie was automatically running through the function checklist as she checked cabin and galley supplies, cabin condition, lighting and lavatories. When she was sure that all was ready, she checked with her agent for early boarding. Soon, she and Doris were busy directing passengers to their seats, hanging up coats, and making a passenger count in the cabin they were responsible for. When the numbers tallied correctly, Doris checked and locked the door.

While Stephanie was busy in the first class section, Doris and May were checking overhead racks and carry-on baggage under seats, securing their equipment, distributing magazines, pillows and blankets, and taking beverage cards when applicable. While May checked seat belts and cautioned passengers to watch for the no smoking sign, Doris and Stephanie were checking seating of unticketed children and sizing up the physical qualifications of passengers sitting by emergency exits. They also checked the physical condition of their jump seats. May made a last minute check of the lavatories to make sure no one was in them during takeoff, and Doris started the taxi-out public announcement.

"Welcome aboard Southaire's continuing service to New York. Your flight attendants for this portion of your journey are Ms. Saranata in the forward cabin, Ms. Phillips in the center cabin and I am Ms. Russell. We will do everything possible to make your flight with us enjoyable. To comply with federal regulations, we ask you to observe the no-smoking sign, fasten your seat belts and straighten your seats for takeoff. Ms. Saranata and Ms. Phillips will demonstrate the oxygen system and show you where emergency exits are located. There is a card describing safety features of this aircraft in the seat pocket in front of you. Material in this pocket is complimentary and you may take it with you when you depart."

Giving the flying time and altitude from information received from her Captain, Doris concluded her announcements as the jets hit full thrust for takeoff and she scurried to the jump seat for a smooth takeoff.

The three attendants began cabin service as soon as the seat belt light was turned off. Stephanie had discovered she had Madame Isabella Leuchendia, the opera star from La Ventanada aboard. Two male attendants hovered about the Madam as soon as the seat belt light went off. As Stephanie made a periodic check of cabin lighting, temperature and started determining beverage choices, one of the prima donna's male companions tossed a mink muff at Stephanie. "Here, mith, put this with Madam's valuable coat you hung in your little, bitty closet."

As Stephanie turned to put away the fur, the second male companion asked, "What do you have to drink, sweetie?"

Realizing she had to start some place for the beverage service, Stephanie reeled off the whole bar selection.

"Okay, sweetie, I'll have a gin and tonic."

Stephanie faced the next man. "Would you care for a drink, sir?"

"I don't know mith, what do you have?"

Taking a deep breath, Stephanie again verbalized the drinks available.

"I'll have a scotch and water, mith."

Leaning toward Madam Leuchendia, Stephanie inquired, "Can I get you a beverage?"

The heavily made-up face turned toward Stephanie and questioned, "What do you have, darling?"

With short, crisp sentences of joyful irritation, Stephanie said, "We have for your pleasure multiple beverages. Included are . . ." and she repeated for the third time . . . "bourbon and branch, Bloody Mary, bourbon on the rocks, bourbon cola, bourbon Collins, daiquiri, Manhattan, mint julep, scotch mist, old fashioned, sours, scotch and water or soda, stinger, martini, gin and tonic, vodka and juices, or any drink on the rocks."

Madam Leuchendia wrinkled her nose at Stephanie. "What would you suggest, darling?"

Stephanie looked at the opera star and her retinue. She smiled gracefully and with eyes sparkling she answered, "Hemlock!"

Turning her back on remarks, "Well, I never!" . . . "Oh, madam, that uncouth creature" . . . "That little snip!" Stephanie felt great. She could imagine what Doris would have said.

As she busied herself in the galley, Steph imagined the conversation with Doris.

Doris would surely say, Steph, when you work in a job like this, you have to expect some people to be double burdens. You shouldn't show your anger in public. You just have to put up with it in this job.

Steph would reply, *Why the hell do I have to put up with it? I don't have to put up with that kind of rudeness in any kind of job. Rude people are just rude people. New York to Miami people are the worst.*

To which Doris would reply, *Stephanie, I can see you now at a P. T. A. meeting.*

Steph would answer, *Doris, you're just too nice. You just lie down and play doormat. I like you but you make me so mad some time because you're always too nice, too sweet, too much of a doormat.*

And Doris would surely say, *Steph, all you need to do is get married, have a good man and your rough edges will wear off.*

To which Steph would remark, *Doris, you're just too nice. You've been downtrodden too long. You've got to stand up for yourself.*

Stephanie smiled as she finished the tray of drinks and ended the imaginary conversation. She knew it by heart. She and Doris had played it out in a running game for the past six months or so that they had flown together. Both went about doing the very same job, going on in their same routes, not wavering a bit from their respective arguments.

In a short time, the flight attendants were concluding their in-flight duties by returning coats, checking overhead racks for personal items, making public announcements, checking lavatories to be sure they were empty, checking for seat belts, cautioning about no-smoking and buckling themselves into their assigned position jump seats. May Phillips made the taxi-in announcement, Doris unlocked the door on signal, and the attendants took positions to bid passengers good-bye.

After a check for any problems or suggestions for flight reports, Stephanie completed the cabin discrepancy log, finished the flight reports and recorded the time on their time cards. Then as the senior agent boarded, they gave him the okay signal and deplaned.

May bid them farewell and took a cab heading for her sister's home for a visit, while Stephanie and Doris climbed into the crew car to head for the hotel. The women objected to the one disadvantage of this particular rotation—that they had an overnight in New York City on the first day . . . the day when they were hardly tired at all. However, the second day of the rotation was a hard day, going from New York to Miami, back to New York and home late the next night into Atlanta . . . and there was no overnight.

After settling in the room, Steph suggested a first run movie.

"No, not tonight. I've got to call George and then I'd just like to order dinner sent to the room," Doris countered.

"You've always got to call George. Honestly, Doris, sometime I wonder how he ever let you get back into flying."

"Aw, Steph. I like to call George. He's expecting it and it makes him feel good. And he didn't let me get back into flying. We discussed it and prayed about it and had many hours of thinking about it before I ever submitted my application for rehire."

"I know. I know. Call your precious George and then let's get something to eat."

During the conversation, Doris said, "Well honey, your clean underwear is stacked on top of the dryer. I'm sorry I didn't get it in your drawer, but things were pretty hectic before I left home. Kimberly had to be picked up from her music lesson, and Mark had to have poster paper for school tomorrow, and I was doing the best I could to take care of everyone before I left."

Stephanie was sitting cross legged on the other twin bed making no bones about her eavesdropping. She rolled her eyes and shook her head.

"George, check Kimberly's temperature tonight before bedtime. She was complaining about a headache." She listened a moment, then turned slightly away from Stephanie and lowered her voice. "Now George, we discussed all possibilities before I ever took this job. I realize she needs her mother if she is truly sick, but I will be home tomorrow night and I'm sure it is nothing to worry about. Yes, George, you know our children come first."

Stephanie threw up her hands. "Hoo boy!"

Doris's conversation over the phone with George continued. "I know I'm a long way from home, Honey . . . I agree, it sounds like Kim might be coming down with something and I feel the same way you do about her staying at home by herself all day tomorrow, but George, there is nothing I can do about it."

She turned to give Stephanie a slight shrug of her shoulders, then returned to the conversation.

"George, quit worrying. I'll see you all tomorrow night. Yes, I'll call if I'm going to be late. Yes, I'll turn on my CB radio when I get in my car so I can contact you if I have any problems. Honestly, honey, you're like radar with the CB. You track my every moment. I think it's really more your toy than my protection." With a few more words of endearment, she bid her family goodnight.

As soon as she hung up, Stephanie pounced on her.

"Why are so submissive to your husband on the phone? You've got to stand up for yourself, Doris. Why were you apologizing for not getting the damn underwear in his drawer? Tell him to find it himself, and if he doesn't like it, he can wash it himself."

'Stephanie, you didn't by any chance happened to hear our conversation, did you?"

Unabashed, Stephanie replied, "Your whole way of thinking is ridiculous." As she continued her woman's cause speech, she changed from her restrictive uniform to a comfortable red robe.

Patiently, Doris confronted her friend. "Steph, marriage really has got a lot going for it. You ought to try it."

Stephanie tightened her robe sash emphatically. "I'd live with a man, but I wouldn't marry him."

Doris frowned as Stephanie continued. "I'd lose too much. The marriage contract takes too much away from a woman, as far as legal ramifications and recourse. There are still a lot of old fuddy-dud laws that have to be changed before marriage can really be a partnership".

"Marriage shouldn't be considered a business partnership. It should be love and contentment and harmony without worrying about the legal ramifications. I married George for pure enjoyment, not as a business transaction."

"Doris, I just don't think you've gotten today's message. You still have old-fashioned ideas."

"I don't think it's so bad to like marriage and to like one's husband and to be liked in return. George and I have a few problems, but we're working them out. It would be boring if it was all smooth going, and it's a comfort to know George is at home worrying about me. It makes me want to hurry and end a trip to get home to him and the children."

Doris was removing her uniform as she talked. "Don't misunderstand, Steph, I like flying. I've always thought being a flight attendant was about the greatest thing that could happen to a girl. It's a terrific job and we are putting a good bit of the money I earn aside to give the kids a college education. Besides, George and I really enjoy the passes I get and we've had some fabulous vacations . . . some that we never would have had, had I not returned to flying. But if it meant breaking up our home or not being married to George, then this job would be the first thing to go, and there would never be a second thought about it."

Steph argued, "Yeah, but you're having both and aren't you finding that both fill a need within you?"

Doris pulled a neat, pink ruffled robe from her suitcase and slipped it on. "Sure. But George and the kids fit my most innermost need. George is growing and learning and making adjustments to my needs as I'm making adjustments to his. We're progressing together. But I'm telling you, Steph, if I absolutely had to make a choice, it would be marriage, period!"

"To each her own. Let's order some food. Maybe you can live on love, but I'm a busy activist and I gotta have fuel. Want a cocktail? I brought a couple of the little bottles from beverage service and we can get a mixer from the hotel."

"Sure, why not. I'll take whatever you have. I'm not particular. I really don't have a favorite drink."

"You should! Everybody should have a very favorite and be able to have exactly that, whenever they want it!"

Early the next morning the two friends started their crisscross day of jetting between New York, Miami and New York and eventually home to Atlanta. As they signed in on the crew sheet, Stephanie let out a moan.

"Drat. We've got Hungry Horace in second seat. He drives me up the wall. He's not just hungry for ordinary things like food and sex and the sports section. He's hungry for everything, a woman's soul, the whole body, the gray roots of a person's brain, everything. He wants to devour people. Ugh, what a way to start this day!"

Doris tried to sooth her. "Just don't go to the cockpit. Keep away from him and don't let him bother you. I'll take up crew coffee and meals. Just don't let him get to you."

When the crew came aboard, Hungry headed straight for Stephanie. "You're here for my pleasure, Sis. Keep it in mind and we'll have our pleasure in a little while. I'm a charter member of the mile-high club and it's time to initiate you. You're looking terrific as always, but then that's because I'm always looking out for you."

"Don't call me sis. I'm not your sister. By the way, I see you still haven't cured your dandruff."

He automatically brushed a hand through his thinning hair. "Baby, I'm not calling you Sis because of kinship, I'm calling you that because of your initials, Ms. Stephanie Irene Saranata, and besides, your father calls you that. I enjoyed flying with Old Mac and if he can call you Sis, then so can I. C'mon up to the cockpit and see what I have for you today."

"If it's one of your sloppy kisses, I'll pass."

"You don't know what you're passing up, Sis." He puckered his lips and gave several simulated kisses to the air as she whirled to keep from striking him and strode briskly down the aisle of the DC-10.

She joined Doris and three other flight attendants for a briefing session by the A-line stewardess. After completing their task cards, Stephanie and Doris went forward to work first class.

Stephanie complained to Doris as they worked efficiently alongside one another. "Hungry started in on his usual trivia. Honest to Pete, he must think I'm Mount Everest and he just has to climb me."

Doris consoled her. "He only picks on you because he knows he bothers you. Just ignore him. He always makes a play for you because you're a tall, good looking girl and he . . . "

"He's a short, fat, slob with dandruff and rummy eyes. Copilots ought to be checked for other things as well as flying ability. Yuk!"

The interphone handset next to the jump seat sounded from the cockpit. Hungry specifically asked that Stephanie come to the cockpit. Doris replaced the receiver and told her co-worker. "I'll go and see what's up. You don't have to go just because he wants you to."

"Naw. I'll do it. Today might just be the perfect opportunity to stomp on him once and for all."

Inside the cockpit, Hungry hassled Stephanie, making her the brunt of his jokes. The whole crew was joining in the laughter. Stephanie was steaming but kept herself in control. Determined to watch the fools waste their valuable time, she stuck it out as long as she felt could afford to waste a little company time. After a couple of minutes she noticed the fatherly looking Captain seemed quieter than the others. After one heated exchange of barbs, the Captain interrupted protectively. "Leave her alone. Stop picking on this little lady."

Stephanie turned on him indignantly. "I don't need you running around playing knight in shinning armor. Save that act for helpless old ladies and little kids. I can look out for myself." She whirled and departed the confines of the cockpit, disgusted with men in Southaire's flying uniforms. As she closed the door, she thumbed her nose at their backs.

The passengers were boarding and Stephanie joined Doris to check boarding passes. An exotically dressed, bearded young man handed Stephanie an envelope. She took it and asked for his boarding pass. He motioned toward the envelope. A line of anxious passengers stood behind him. Assuming he probably didn't speak English, Stephanie pulled him aside to stand by her while she continued to check boarding passes.

When the boarding ensemble was down to a trickle, Stephanie smiled at the non-vocal young man and removed the typed sheet from his envelope. She quickly scanned the paper, then incredulously read it again more slowly.

Hi there, Stewardess. I am a friendly stow-away trying to get to Phoenix where my lady is about to give birth to my heir. I will sit quietly, make no waves, ask not for one morsel of food, nor request one sip of beverage. I will not communicate our little secret to a single other person aboard this aircraft. When we reach our destination, I will mingle quickly with deplaning passengers and before this trip is over, you will not remember that I was ever aboard your equipment. Signed, Your Friendliest Stow-away Ever.

Without raising her voice, Stephanie advised him. "You're proposing that I commit a federal offense by letting you on board without a ticket. I suggest you deplane at once and I hope that I will forget this incident. I hardly believe it now."

A smile crinkled his pleading features and she realized he was not quite as young as she had first thought. His voice was soft. "Think of it for a moment, fair maiden. Perchance you will have a change of conscience."

"Perchance I won't. You get off and purchase a ticket, or I'll notify our Agent and have you removed."

He waved a hand toward the cabin and said, "I can see you've boarded everyone booked for this flight and you've still got empty seats. So who's it going to hurt to let me have one of them? The airline won't lose any money. Besides, I have a right to fly in public air space. The sky belongs to everybody and you've got seats here that nobody is riding in.

So who are you to tell me I should have bought a ticket to sit in one of these seats?"

She started looking for the Southaire Agent. Walking toward the boarding area, the stowaway trailed her retreating figure. His voice rose. "I have a right. You can't say I can't fly in this plane. The government has subsidized airlines. Your prices are fixed! Capitalistic! Monopolistic! You haven't got any business telling me I can't go to Phoenix."

He was shouting while Stephanie explained to the airline representative. Two on duty guards were summoned and the dreamer was forcefully helped toward the Federal Aviation Agency office of the airport.

When Stephanie returned to the cabin, Doris inquired, "What was that all about?"

Stephanie shrugged. "Some character who saw the movie *Airport* too many times." She slipped a gaily printed tunic apron over her head. Completing on ground duties, and taxi-out chores, the flight attendants were soon busy serving in the air.

James Squires was a bit apprehensive about flying and was quick to tell Doris when he stopped her in the aisle to re-order a second drink to help reinforce his courage. Soon he stopped her again, whispered his question and she whispered pointed directions. The portly gentleman rose unsteadily and made his way to the lavatory. While passenger Squires was inside the tiny room, the DC-10 encountered some jostling air turbulence. In a few moments, a white-faced, panic-eyed James Squires grabbed at Doris when she walked by while checking seat belts. He started stammering.

"I . . . I was pretty nervous in there. It's . . . it's pretty small, ya know, and . . . and . . . and the damn light was on about returning to your seat, and we hit the bump and . . . and . . . and anyway, I lost my glasses, uh, my spectacles landed in the john, and, uh, what can be done? I'm going to a business meeting, and I can't see anything without my glasses. They're bifocals! Miss, I gotta have those glasses!"

Doris looked inside the lavatory. "I don't see any glasses, sir."

Urgently he said, "They're not in a visible place, Miss."

"Are you sure they went down there? Could you have left them at your seat? You've had a few drinks and you're pretty excited, Mr. Squires."

"Nope! I'm positive. We hit that little bit of rough air and my wife kept telling me I should have gotten them tightened, but they're there, miss, right where I said they were! What are you going to do? I've got to have my glasses."

Doris grabbed at Stephanie as she approached them. Quickly Doris explained the problem. Stephanie replied, "Why are you telling me this? I'm a flight attendant, not a plumber."

Doris and Stephanie conferred. "I remember hearing about a lady who lost a diamond ring one time. They got it out after the flight was on the ground."

Squires interrupted their conversation with, "No ma'am. I can't wait that long. Besides, I'm being met and being taken directly to the meeting when this flight lands in Miami. A whole corporation depends on me getting there on time. I can't wait for them to fish around on the ground. I gotta have my bifocals now. I've got business briefs to review on this flight."

The girls looked blankly at him. He continued, "They haven't cleared the pipes or anything yet. They're just right down there. I didn't flush it yet!"

Stephanie gave him a sad look. "We can't put our hands down there right now. We're in the midst of serving food. Our hands are already sterilized for meal service."

"Do you have anything that would reach down there?"

Doris was sympathetic. "No, sorry. Can't think of anything."

"How about your Captain? Would he know how to solve this problem?" James' bald head was dotted with drops of perspiration.

172 *Marty Ruffin Gardner*

Stephanie snapped her fingers and declared, "Our Captain might not, but I'll bet I know how to get the problem solved."

A grateful James grabbed her arm and exclaimed, "Oh, I hope so."

Stephanie winked at Doris as she said, "I'll go get Officer H. Harris."

Doris rolled her eyes. "Oh Stephanie!"

Turning to Mr. Squires, Doris urged him to return to his seat. "We'll do what we can to help."

"Would it be possible to get one more drink?"

"In this case, I think it would be possible."

While Doris prepared the drink, Stephanie went to the cockpit. Turning on all her charm, she told Hungry, "We really do need you. I guess you're right after all. This is one situation we poor females just can't handle. I thought women could handle everything, but this problem has convinced me that you're right. You're the only one I know qualified to do the job. You're cut out for it."

Puffing up to his full five foot six, Harris straightened his tie and told the Captain he would go back and take care of the problem for the girls.

Stephanie preceded Hungry and stopped beside passenger Squires without telling Officer Harris the nature of the problem. She addressed Mr. Squires. "Sir, we have your problem solved. Officer Harris here has volunteered to retrieve your glasses out of the toilet."

Hungry tried not to look upset in front of all the passengers who were now smiling at him with admiration. He realized he didn't have any choice but to roll up his sleeves and get to work.

Loudly, Stephanie said, "Oh, thank you, Officer Harris, I knew this was a job only you could do!"

Stephanie was weary by the time she reached her apartment late that evening in Atlanta, but as always, she got a fresh burst of energy when she opened the door.

Her apartment suited her perfectly. Books dominated the living area piled on homemade brick and board shelves, and a South American decor was testimony to Stephanie's years of teaching high school Spanish. Furniture was sparse, mostly odds and ends that she had picked up a flea markets and borrowed from her folks. Magazines were stacked against one wall. There was one comfortable chair facing a small black and white TV given to her by a friend who was moving. It was a small, efficiency apartment, filling Stephanie's needs without draining her bank account.

Her phone rang just as she was grabbing an apple from the fridge. With a mouth full of apple, she mumbled, "Lo, oh, hi Mac! Where are you?"

McLain Saranata's voice boomed over the instrument. "Hey, honey. How's my favorite broad? When ya coming down to see yer Mom and me?"

"Aw, Pop, you know how it is." She took another chomp from the apple. "You in town?"

"Yeah, Babe. I come up fer a radio equipment demo at the merchandise mart. Tandy Corp's got out a new model I'm kinda interested in."

"How's the best air charter business in Florida these days? You making lots of money?" She kicked off her shoes.

"Naw, but I'm having good time. When ya gonna quit this stew business and come fly fer ya own father? I'll give ya a job any times ya wants it, Sis."

"Thanks, but no thanks. I'm going to be a pilot for South-aire. I'm going to take over the seat you vacated when you retired, Pop. You ought to come fly with me sometime, Pop. I passed my instrument exam last month."

After receiving a noncommittal grunt, she asked, "Is Mom with you?" Stephanie took another chomp from her apple.

"Naw! That skirts got so much going she don't have time to travel wid me. She's leading a seminar on senior citizen rights, ya know, her Gray Panther group, Those old skirts is having a meeting and Pauline's in charge of it. Those old gals are running around picketing and making speeches and all that bunk. Ain't got a bit of sense, and yer Mom's right in there in the middle of it. She's always doing something."

Listening to the inflection in his voice, Stephanie chided her father, "And you think she's just great for doing it, don't you? Mom's always had you right where you should be and you know it. How long are you going to be in town?"

"Few days. Ya gonna buy me dinner?"

"Sho nuff, Pop. I'll meet you in an hour. You at the Ambassador?"

"Where else? Put on a dress, Sis, don't wear none of those pants things. I don't like to see a gal in trousers. Ain't right, women wearing pants all the time."

Stephanie donned a tailored brown denim pants suit and ran a brush through her wiry hair before she left to meet Mac. The father and daughter visit was pleasant even though he glared at her pants suit, and their bantering camaraderie was as warm as ever. Mac asked Stephanie again during dinner to consider giving up being a stewardess and coming to fly as one of his pilots for his airline charter service in Sarasota. They parted with her promising to think it over.

Chapter 20—Our ETA is Roast Beef

Stephanie had been needling Doris about her domestic tranquility before they picked up the connecting flight in Atlanta. Doris had been unusually pensive and only answering with an "uh huh" occasionally because she was thinking seriously about her situation. She felt perhaps the younger generation had something worthwhile to say to her more stoic age group. Among the passengers was a wrinkled suited man with his shirt collar unbuttoned and tie askew who appeared to be near her own age. He had waved a greeting to the new group of attendants as they boarded the L-1011 jet aircraft.

As Doris walked by, he grabbed her hand. "Hey Chicken Little, I've been waiting for you to board. If you need any help on the L-eleven-eleven, you just let me know. I fly all the time and I help you attendants quite a bit." He gave her a comrade's wink.

Doris smiled and replied as she gently disengaged her hand. "Why thank you, sir. If there are any problems aboard our L-ten-eleven today, we will notify you."

"Heh, heh, I meant to say L-ten-eleven." He looked out the window as Doris continued with her duties.

After the three Rolls Royce engines had lifted the aircraft to its cruising speed of 550 MPH, the ten Flight Attendants started meal service. Doris was waiting by the galley lift for a service cart when she felt a slap on her back. She whirled around.

"Hi there! I just sauntered over to see if you need me to help you."

It was the man who had grabbed her hand. Startled, she replied, "Oh no, thank you. Not yet. I'll let you know if we do. Perhaps you might go to your seat. Meal service is pretty hectic."

"Chicken Little, you don't have to worry about me. I'm used to a hectic life. I'm president of my own company and you know what kind of life that means. I do a lot of business with all the airlines and I know all about your fast meal services."

Doris eyed him as he was talking. His suit was flashily cheap and badly wrinkled. The pointed toes of his shoes were scuffed. He was a little rough looking around the edges. Doris felt sorry for him.

"I'm sure you are quite a tycoon and I'm glad we have you on board today, but you really would be doing me a tremendous favor if you would return to your seat and get ready for your dinner." She beamed a smile.

"Okay, Chicken Little. One thing I've learned, you gals are the boss on this plane when it comes to us business men. We admire the way you work and you do make a trip enjoyable."

"You're very kind. Ooops, here is my service cart. Excuse me."

"I've got an important appointment in Vegas as soon as we arrive. By the way, do you know our EAT yet?"

Giving him her sweetest smile, she replied, "We're going to EAT roast beef."

"I'm going to my seat, Miss."

"By the way, our ETA is 6:50."

Doris couldn't suppress a naughty smile as she checked her tray. One thought kept crowding in. *I can't wait to tell Stephanie how I handled that man.* When they had a minute to chat, Doris related the know-it-all passenger experience and smugly emphasized her reply to the man. "I've been around you too long, Stephanie Saranata, 'cause I'm starting to sound like you."

"From the grin on your face, I can tell you're not too upset about it. You're learning. There's hope for you yet, Doris."

On their next rotation trip from Miami to Detroit, a bulging Mrs. Mary Anne Troy boarded. Stephanie inquired, "When is your baby due?"

She patted her gingham covered belly answering, "Oh not for three more weeks. It's a good thing I have a little more time because we're in the process of moving to Detroit. My husband and our other three children are driving there now and plan to meet me. We just felt like the automobile trip would be too much for me in my condition, so I'm the lucky one. I get to fly."

With boarding passengers behind her, the mother-to-be moved slowly on down the aisle. Stephanie called after her. "If you need anything, let us know."

Stephanie was flying senior to the four attendant crew, and when the last passenger was boarded, the agent gave her the clearance and other dispatch forms. While the agent closed the door, Doris checked it, and then went ahead with her duties. Stephanie took the paperwork to the cockpit, then went to the forward buffet and started the taxi-out public announcement. While she extolled the features of Southaire jet service, the other attendants demonstrated oxygen masks and pointed to the appropriate seat and bulkhead. They explained emergency equipment, and then demonstrated how to wear life preservers as they moved into various sections of the cabin.

Stephanie's voice declared, "Good morning. It's our pleasure to welcome you on board Southaire's jet flight 307 to Detroit with an intermediate stop in Atlanta. Our flight today is under the command of Captain Burmister. Flight attendants are Mrs. Russell, Miss Sermon, Miss Freeman, and I am Miss Saranata. We would like to take a few moments now to acquaint you with the interior of this DC-8 equipment. No smoking and fasten seat belt signs are on panels in both cabins. Please observe these when they are illuminated as they are at this time. Emergency exits are being pointed to by the cabin attendants. In the seat pocket in front of you, you will find a card describing safety features on this aircraft. We do ask you to check over this while we taxi out. As on all jet equipment, we are equipped with an automatic oxygen system. Masks similar to those your flight attendants are demonstrating are located under panels overhead. In the unlikely event of decompression, these panels will open automatically revealing several masks. Should this occur, it is your responsibility to reach up, pull the mask the entire length of the tubing, place the gold cup over nose and mouth and breathe normally. Smoking is not permitted when oxygen is in use. Now, in preparation for takeoff in accordance with Federal Aviation Agency requirements, please return your seat back and tray to their up-right and locked positions. We hope you enjoy your flight with us today."

As she clicked the off switch, all attendants proceeded to their specified seats for takeoff, seats that were situated near exits for which they would be responsible in the event of an emergency.

As soon as the seat belt sign was turned off, the group went into their pattern of smooth teamwork, determining meal and beverage service for their 195 passengers. Doris did a periodic check of cabin lighting, temperature and checked the lavatories. As she passed by the pregnant woman, Doris softly inquired, "Doing okay?"

Mrs. Troy's brown curls clung damply around her pale face. "I'm having a few twitches here and there but nothing that I can't stand until we get to Detroit. Ya know, I told the other flight attendant this is a company transfer for my husband, and he and our kids and all our furniture and even our family dog are on their way. I would have preferred to wait to make such a major move until after this baby was born, but when you work for a big company and they say move, well, you move."

"If you get too uncomfortable, we have some aspirin. Here, I'll place this pillow behind you. Perhaps it will help. Hope you enjoy your meal."

"Thank you. You're very kind."

Stephanie didn't pay much attention to the conversation three young fellows were having as she smiled her way past their coach seats.

"She'll never change this. We'll get 'em free. Ya just gotta know how to make out in the world today. Shush. Here she comes. Ah, miss! We'd like, uh, a drink, uh, three drinks. We want whisky sours, uh, yeah, three whisky sours. Yeah, bring us three super dooper Southaire whisky sours . . .right away!"

She gave them the benefit of her long black eyelashes as she fluttered them coquettishly. "Certainly gentlemen. Drinks are $2.00 each. Your whisky sours will cost $6.00 in advance."

The loud talking fellow in the middle seat slowly withdrew his French style monogrammed wallet and extracted a $100 bill. With youthful aplomb he bragged, "It's the smallest I have." As Stephanie reached for the bill, he nudged his companion on his left.

Her dazzling smile beamed. "Thank you. I'll bring your change with your drinks, sir." The men exchanged disgusted looks.

In the galley, Stephanie pushed the cockpit intercom. The pilots booming voice made the instrument unnecessary. "Yeah, Chick, what's your problem?"

"Some damn fool gave a hundred dollar bill for three drinks."

"And you want us to come to your rescue with change? What makes you think pilots are so all fired rich? We got mortgages, mistresses, fur-hungry wives and kids needing braces."

"Ya got the money or you don't? In case you don't know, this is a super DC-8. We got 195 booze thirsty folks. We're cruising 575 miles per hour and if we're gonna get 'em all bombed before Detroit, I gotta hurry."

"Comin' at ya, Doll. We may have to do some circling. Atlanta's socked in right now. We'll know more in an hour and we'll keep ya posted."

An attendant call button sounded and Stephanie looked around for one of the others to answer, but they were all occupied so she went into the cabin to answer the summons. Mary Ann Troy, the pregnant woman, was perspiring and moaning softly. The male passenger seated next to her was wiping her brow with his handkerchief and sighed with relief when Stephanie appeared.

"What's wrong, Mrs. Troy? Are you in pain?" Her eyes widened as she thought of a sudden possibility. "You aren't having labor pains!" Mary Ann nodded apologetically, and then stiffened with the onset of another contraction. "Uh, hang on. Try to relax. I'll see if there is a doctor on board." Stephanie tried to smile comfortingly.

The male passenger beside Mrs. Troy got up. "I'll move out of the way. Is there any other seat I can have?"

"For the moment, the best I can offer is my attendant jump seat up front if you don't mind just sitting up there for a few minutes. I'll see if we have a doctor aboard."

On her way to the galley, Stephanie encountered Doris who started to hand her a fistful of dollar bills. Stephanie pointed and said, "The three guys in row 28. They're supposed to get $94.00 change. I've got their hundred dollar bill in my pocket. Mrs. Troy's having problems."

Stephanie hurried to the public address system. Her voice sounded worried as she paged for a doctor, a nurse or a paramedic on board. There was no response. When she repeated the request for the third time there was still no help forthcoming. Doris stood quietly beside her.

Stephanie asked, "Have you seen her yet, have you seen Mrs. Troy?"

"Yes. She's in hard labor. We've got a lot to do in a very short time."

"Do you know what to do? If you don't, then I think I do. I've read magazines and studied about natural childbirth."

"I guess I'm experienced. I have two children." Doris plugged in the water filled coffee pot. "Better get one of the other attendants in here to keep boiling water, refilling this pot and bring it to me. Notify the cockpit to call ahead for an ambulance in Atlanta."

"We may not land in Atlanta. Socked in."

"Oh, Lord! Well, I'm going to move her to the front seat by the buffet and make her a bed on the floor. I'll need some help hanging blankets around to give her some privacy. Hopefully the baby won't be born before we can land but her water has already broken. Help me pray. If we ever needed divine guidance, we need it now. Dear Lord, help us all."

As Doris gathered the supplies she would need, Stephanie called to her retreating back, "Tell her to breathe deeply and think calm thoughts."

When Doris reached the seat, she told the attending attendant with Mrs. Troy, "Help me get her moved up to the seats by the buffet. Spread blankets on the floor and put down several pillows. Try to hang some blankets from the overhead rack. Move as many people around as you can and ask them to double up. I realize we can't land that way, but for the time being, she shouldn't be stared at by a curious crowd."

When preparations were completed, Mrs. Troy's labor pains were timed. They were two minutes apart. The copilot called from outside the curtained area, "Doris is there anything I can do?"

"How's your midwife training?"

"Not up to par but I'm willing to help."

"Ask Stephanie. She's in charge of giving orders."

Doris turned her attention to her patient. "Mrs. Troy, try not to bear down just yet. Everything is being done to ensure your safety. We've arranged for an ambulance when we land. Take a sip of this water. Outside the curtained area, Stephanie was cracking orders out like a drill sergeant. To the helpful copilot she ordered, "Go scrub your hands with soap. Use a brush. Make sure you get a good lather."

"But I don't have a brush."

"You've got a toothbrush, haven't you? Use that. Remember to work up a good lather and scrub all the way up your arms to your elbows. Hurry!" To one of her fellow coworkers, she commanded, "Keep boiling water, lots of hot water is needed."

"But we're running out of things to put the hot water in."

"Put it in a burp bag. We need lots of hot water. Hurry!" Leaving her command post in the center cabin, Stephanie poked her head inside the blanketed reserve. "Breathe deeply, uh oh. Doris? DORIS!!"

"Shush! The baby's coming. Keep everyone away. Mrs. Troy is doing fine. Shut the curtain, Stephanie."

Stephanie backed into a junior stewardess attendant holding an armful of napkins and pillow cases who asked her, "Where shall I put these, Stephanie?"

Dazed she answered, "Oh just anyplace. Here, I'll take them." She looked at the pieces of cloth as if she couldn't fathom why there were being handed to her and she said to no one in particular, "But she didn't go through phase two like she is supposed to in natural childbirth. I should have told Mrs. Troy to do phase two."

The copilot reappeared. Both hands were held up in front of his face and water dripped from his elbows. "All set. What do you want me to do?" Stephanie motioned toward the hung blankets.

"Ask Doris, but don't look inside."

"Doris?" he whispered, "Oh, Doris . . . I'm scrubbed. What do you want me to do?"

A tiny piercing wail penetrated his soft inquiry.

Everyone stopped. Then came Doris' answer, "Go back up and land us in Atlanta. Mother and son are okay."

Another cry shattered the quiet atmosphere. Doris' lilting exuberance filtered through the temporary maternity room. "Better make that, mother okay, son a bit unhappy."

Stephanie whirled to the cabin and shouted, "It's a boy! We have a new passenger."

A cheer sounded.

Inside the makeshift delivery room, Doris and Mrs. Troy smiled at each other. The weary mother lifted her head and blew a kiss towards her son. Doris had cleaned off the baby but had left the umbilical cord attached, placing the baby on his mother's abdomen to await the ambulance medical attendants.

Then Doris offered a soft prayer, "Thank you, Lord, for another miracle."

Stephanie and the group around her started chatting. Stephanie pondered aloud, "How do we list him on the passenger manifest? Does Southaire charge him half-fare since he boarded in mid-air?" she joked.

Relief and happiness were reflected in every passenger's expression as the seat belt sign appeared and the flight attendants checked seat belts. The Captain's voice came on the PA system to tell how proud he was of all the cabin attendants, and what an honor it was for Southaire to have the Troy baby born on board. Applause followed his sign-off. Immediately several passengers started telling the flight attendants that the whole group on board were de-facto godparents for that Troy baby. A burp bag collection of money was donated to buy a present for the baby and a large bouquet of flowers for the brave mother. One of the junior attendants accepted it on behalf of the mother and told everyone she would take care of purchasing just exactly what they would have picked out themselves.

Within a week, letters to both Doris and Stephanie appeared in their stewardess' mail boxes. Even though each was a personal letter, the message was the same. The baby had been named Dory Stephen Troy after flight attendants Doris Russell and Stephanie Saranata. That was the closest name the parents could come to for a boy from composites of Doris and Stephanie.

Doris expressed surprise. "Why, I never expected Mr. and Mrs. Troy to do anything this fine. That's awfully nice of them."

Stephanie became sentimental. "Ya know, someday I might just want to have a baby. I've never had anything named for me before. It's rather touching."

In the middle of March, 1974, Stephanie and Doris picked up a charter DC-stretch 8 jet from Cincinnati to Nassau along with four other Atlanta based flight attendants. Burnham Tours made all the arrangements and Joe Burnham, owner, was accompanying the group of senior citizens. It was to be three days and two nights in exotic Nassau. The flight attendants and pilots were privileged to have the same layover time so they could also work the charter back when the mini-vacation was over.

From the beginning, Joe Burnham proved to be a griping, never-satisfied tour director. He was out of context with his delightful clients, some of whom were first riders, and most of whom had saved for years to take this last fling of a vacation. His faded red blazer with a gold "B" embroidered on the pocket was visible in the center of every problem.

He rankled Stephanie whenever he got a chance and as soon as they were airborne, she told Doris, "I don't give a damn if I am A-line stewardess for this trip. You take care of Joe Blow. He's really getting to me and we gotta be nice for three days. He may be tour boss, but I am boss of this cabin, and if he keeps on with his bitching, one of us is going to lose our seniority."

"Okay, Steph. Will do. But aren't these people sweet?"

The attendants started the beverage and meal service. Since the charter was commissioned as economy class, sandwiches and light garnishments with cola or tea were planned. About midway during the meal service for the 191 passengers, Joe Burnham started raising a ruckus. As he marched up and down the aisle, he shouted to the attendants, "What, what are you serving my people? I distinctly remember ordering steak for everyone." He turned back and forth to the passengers and shouted. "You people should be eating steak. You paid for steak. I'm going to sue Southaire. Crummy outfit! This is your hard earned money that you paid for deluxe service and what do you get? Sandwiches! I'll see about this."

He confronted one of the junior attendants. "Who's in charge of this? Who signs for your meals? Who's the chief honcho of this group?"

The girl pointed to Stephanie.

He roared toward her. Keeping his voice loud so surrounding passengers would be sure to hear, he demanded, "Will you tell me why my people are eating sandwiches when they should be having steak?"

Stephanie had already flipped through her in-flight service forms when he first started the commotion. She was ready for him. In a matching loud voice, she countered as she handed him a signed meal request form from her dispatch papers. "Because sandwiches are what you ordered, sir."

"What do you mean, I ordered? My people paid me personally for steak on this charter."

She pointed to the signature on the meal authorization form. "Is that your name, Joe Burnham?" Loudly she announced. "It so states that you desire economy service on this charter, that you personally chose the types of sandwiches and all food and beverage supplies for this flight, that you in fact paid economy prices for an economy charter. If that is not your handwriting, then someone is running around signing your name to legal, binding documents."

"Yes, that's my signature, but there must be a mistake, I didn't know what I was signing."

"You had to know. You ordered the types of sandwiches. One thing in your favor, Mr. Burnham, at least you did order meat and not peanut butter and jelly. For this, your people can thank you."

"Well, perhaps I was thinking of another tour I arranged."

She looked at him in disgust, and then took the paper from his hands saying, "Perhaps."

Doris was near Mr. And Mrs. Dunhart and leaned slightly over them to inquire if they would like anything else before she removed their tray. Mrs. Dunhart timid idly inquired, "My dear, I hate to bother you, but I was wondering about something. Where are the propellers?"

Pausing a moment, Doris answered, "Mrs. Dunhart, this is a DC-8. It has four fan jet engines manufactured by Pratt and Whitney. With the jets, we don't need propellers. In case you are interested, the wing span is almost 140 feet and the height at the tail is over 42 feet high."

Isabel Dunhart's eyes widened. "Oh, my! Henry, did you hear? My dear would you repeat that so I can write it down. I must tell our grandchildren. Also, is it alright if I have these things in this little seat pocket. It says complimentary on them. I want to take them home for our grandchildren. This is the first time Henry and I have ever flown. Henry is a barber and has his one shop near the Covington airport, although the grow hair tonics didn't do Henry much good as you can tell from his bald head."

Doris repeated the measurements. "We're cruising at 35,000 feet and traveling about 600 miles per hour. Of course you're welcome to take everything that says complimentary with you. If there are some things in your packet that you would like more of, you just let me know."

"Well, what about Henry's and my drinking cups, these little cups that have Southaire printed on them. Are they disposable?"

"They certainly are. We discard them when we get the trays to the buffet area. Would you like to have some?

"My dear, I would be so grateful."

Doris winked. "I'll get you a whole set, a clean set. Now how about a pillow to make you more comfortable? How about you, Mr. Dunhart?"

"Oh no, I wouldn't want to trouble you. Isabel doesn't need one either. She is too excited to sit still. I hope she isn't making a pest of herself to you."

"Not in the least. We're delighted to be serving you. Call if you need anything."

The quiet drone of conversation was interrupted by a woman a few seats behind the Dunharts who began gasping and moaning. By the time Doris reached her, she was clutching her left breast. Seeing Doris, she cried, "I'm having a heart attack, do something . . . quick, quick, help me."

Doris reached over and adjusted the woman's seat to a half-sitting position, then prepared to administer oxygen. She pressed the stewardess call button to summon help.

A slim, tall, graying man two sets further back unwound his long legs from under his seat and approached Doris. In a quiet voice, he reassured her. "I am a doctor. Do you want my help?" Gratefully, Doris nodded. The man asked the terrified woman, "I am a physician, do you want me to treat you?"

She gasped, "Help me, help me."

One of the junior flight attendants had appeared beside Doris and was instructed to fetch the doctor's bag from beneath his seat. He suggested that Doris fix the woman a half cup of warm tea. Upon receiving his bag, he extracted his stethoscope.

He told the flight attendant to unbutton the woman's blouse and as Doris went for the tea, he began listening to the passenger's heart.

When Doris returned, the doctor was sitting beside the woman who lay against a pillow, her eyes closed. He took the tea and held it to her lips. She sipped a few drops then opened her eyes. Seeing Doris, she muttered, "I'm sorry. I panicked. This nice doctor tells me I just have a case of indigestion. I guess I gobbled my sandwich too fast. I was so hungry and was looking forward to a big steak dinner."

Joe Burnham pranced like a puffed up bantam rooster up to the seat. "Is she okay? I was afraid to come up before now. I never had anyone have a heart attack on one of my tours. I would have been ruined if she had died."

The doctor stood up. "It's okay Mr. Burnham. What she has isn't very contagious. Only people who get within five feet of her can catch the disease."

"My gosh man, I'm within five feet of her." He backed up and turning on his heels he hurried toward his seat.

Doris looked up at the doctor's twinkling grin. He said, "I couldn't resist that. He is an obnoxious fellow. If I had known more about him when I answered the newspaper advertisement about this tour, I probably would never have signed up."

"So, that's how you all got together. I was wondering because you didn't seem to know one another and most charters are a group or a club or a sports team."

"There was a very enticing ad in the paper and on TV, and I guess we all answered it because the few that I've talked with so far say that is how they found out about this tour. I guess it's a good deal. He just comes on a bit strong."

"Well, perhaps he has problems that we don't know about, or maybe he's just a perfectionist."

"Or a worry wart." The doctor shrugged. "Well, if Mrs. Stillman has any more problems, let me know. I gave her a couple of pills to take with her tea. She should have a comfortable trip the rest of the way."

"Thank you so very much, Dr. Parker."

In Nassau, the flight attendants and crew stayed as far away from the tour group's activities as possible, mostly soaking up the sun on the beach. Doris was the lone active one. She wanted to spend a lot of time shopping for her family, for her relatives, and even for friends in her neighborhood.

"Please Stephanie, go shopping with me first, then we'll go to the beach with others later on. C'mon, I've just got to get something else for my mother-in-law," Doris begged.

Stephanie moaned, "Why don't you just tell your mother-in-law to go to hell? This is supposed to be a vacation. So vacation!"

Stephanie was asked out for an evening by an author she met at the basket market. Dressed in his cut-off jeans, T-shirt and floppy straw hat, the sociologist and writer had moved down to Nassau for a season to complete work on a new political book. Here, he was able to stroll unrecognized among the natives and most tourists. However, Stephanie recognized him. They started a conversation and he offered to show Stephanie the night life on the island.

"Come on with us, Doris and see the real island life."

Doris replied, "No, you go ahead and have your date."

"It's not a date. You're perfectly welcome to come along. It's not some cozy twosome, you know."

"Run along and have fun. I'm not going to wait up. Don't you want to wear something prettier than those slacks?"

"Now come on Doris, you're hopeless. It's not some big romantic date."

Stephanie returned to their shared room quite, quite late and gave no report about her evening. Doris knew better than to ask. She felt certain Stephanie had been disappointed with her celebrity date. Otherwise, Steph would have come in talking about him and comparing him to Doris's husband, George. Doris knew Steph didn't like George. She also suspected Steph hadn't found many men in her lifetime that she did like. Stephanie was a strong personality and Doris surmised that it would take a giant of a man to really attract and hold Stephanie's love. Doris knew Steph hadn't yet met him, but that she wanted to.

Their vacation was brief and soon they were winging their way back across the great pond homeward. While the attendants were serving, Joe Burnham's red coat was seen moving from seat to seat. He told his charter group, "Be sure and ask the stewardesses for playing cards and when you get through with them, turn them over to me. I'll take care of them. Also, get as many of the little bottles of whisky as you can. I'll collect the unused ones when we get closer to Cincinnati."

Mrs. Dunhart stopped Doris. "Henry and I bought a tiny little souvenir for you to take to your children. You were so nice to show us their pictures and you have been so sweet on this trip."

"Oh Mrs. Dunhart, you shouldn't have done that. Why don't you take these souvenirs to your grandchildren?"

"No, no, my dear. We have other things for our babies. These shells are for your children."

"You are both so kind. You're perfect passengers, and I don't mean just because of these souvenirs, which I am grateful for, but because you are both such sweet people. It really has been a pleasure to have you on Southaire and I sincerely hope I get to be your stewardess again someday. Thank you again for these beautiful shells. My children will be delighted. Can I get you anything?"

As the meal service ended and most of the trays were picked up, the attendants strolled through the cabin visiting with the charter group.

Joe Burnham started passing two empty ice buckets and told groups of passengers within voice range. "Everybody put in two dollars each for the stewardesses who have served us this tour. They have worked hard and done a super job. The least we can do is contribute a nice tip for each of them. C'mon, everybody, put in two dollars. C'mon, it won't break you and these nice girls deserve a little something extra."

As he made his way down the aisle, he would occasionally tell a passing attendant as loudly as possible. "Hey, you gals have done a terrific job. Be sure to tell all your friends about Burnham Travel Tours. I'm thinking of branching out with offices in Atlanta, Miami and Chicago, so you can tell almost every group of passengers that if they want a really good tour director to contact Burnham Tours."

The attendants tried to ignore him. They knew why he was taking up the collection because he made a point of saying loudly in front of them, "Be sure and put in two dollars per person for this outstanding group of hostesses. We gotta reward them."

The main body of the passengers were nice, middle-aged comfortable people. They were weary from having Joe Burnham drag them all over Nassau to see every tourist trap and attraction. He had been a whip cracking taskmaster and his collection for the stewardesses appeared to them to be the first genuine nice thing he had done the entire trip. They were ready to concede that perhaps they had misjudged him when he was at last doing something extraordinary for the girls who had worked very hard to make the trip pleasant.

As the attendants went about their duties, they occasionally heard a grumble or two. "Martha, I don't even think I've got two dollars after the way that guy has drained our pockets." . . . "Sally, you got any money left in your purse. I used my last at the hotel." . . . "Wonder what he's gonna think of next to spend our money on?" . . .

Through it all Joe Burnham kept loudly encouraging, "Dig deep, it's for our charming hostesses."

Once, Stephanie whispered sweetly to Joe as she passed him in the aisle, "We're called attendants, not hostesses."

After the collection buckets were full, Joe went back to his seat to separate the money. He made a big production of making six separate stacks, one for each girl. While the attendants were strolling the cabin, they happened to see him place a bill on each of the stacks, then stuff several bills in his own pocket. They started watching Mr. Burnham a bit closer. Finally Stephanie went into the buffet and started doing some figuring on her own. She called Doris in to join her. "According to my figures with 191 passengers on board, at $2.00 a head, it adds up to $764.00 and divided down into six, we should each get, oh, roughly $127.00."

The head of Burnham Tours made a grand finale production of presenting each attendant with a wad of bills. When they counted their tips, they found they had $25.00 apiece. Stephanie and Doris talked to the others and compared figures.

Stephanie said, "That bird shorted us and gypped those poor people. He's pocketed a bundle. We gotta let them know what's going on."

Doris was sympathetic. "These sweet, adorable people. Some of them hardly had $2.00 left over from this trip. I don't even want to take their money. We should still have the rule that attendants are not allowed to accept tips. I feel bad about this. These poor people . . ."

Stephanie stuck out her chin. "Well, I'm going to do something about it."

She marched to the public address system and clicked it on. "We want to thank you all for the twenty-five dollar gift you have given each of the six of us. Twenty-five dollars for each of us six attendants is very kind of you and we really have enjoyed helping you have a nice trip." She emphasized the numbers as she spoke.

The orange glow of the fasten seat belt sign appeared. While the stewardesses were checking seat belts, several of the passengers inquired, "Is twenty-five dollars all the money you got? We thought you would get more."

The passengers began talking and grumbling among themselves and started leaning forward to talk to their neighbors. Pencils and paper were evident as men and women started calculating figures. Several glanced down the aisle toward Joe Burnham who sat in a back seat. The attendants noticed more and more heads figuring together over pieces of paper as they reconfirmed the fact that the girls had only received $25.00 each. Mumbles were heard. "Leon, check my figures again." . . . "Sarah, I'm tired and this guy has ripped us off again" . . . "Sam, how many different ways do you suppose this Burnham has taken us to the cleaners?" . . .

When the wheels touched down, ending the Nassau charter, Joe Burnham was waiting at the exit door. As soon as the door was opened, he took off running and several middle aged men, with shirttails flapping, took up the chase. Those that viewed the spectacle finally got their money's worth in laughter.

Chapter 21—Uncork your Corkscrew, Stew!

Moments of turbulence jostled the snoozing passengers on a commuter flight into Atlanta. Wisps of fog were reported at ground level, but none of the airports along the route were fogged in. The flight attendants were tired and ready to get to Atlanta and to bed. They had been working since midnight and would be relieved to turn the ship over to a new crew when Atlanta passengers deplaned. Doris looked out the window as they got into the approach pattern and was relieved to see dawn sun peek through the clouds, and to know that in about fifteen more minutes this flight would be logged in as routine. The seat belt sign was on and all passengers were secure.

Abruptly three distinct rings of the interphone call system sounded and then were repeated at two second intervals. Stephanie was closest to the phone. She picked up the instrument.

"Saranata here. What's up?"

The First Officers voice commanded, "Come to the cockpit immediately!"

Unbuckling herself from the jump seat, Stephanie calmly made her way to the cockpit, smiling reassurance at the few passengers who looked at her with raised eyebrows.

When Doris saw Stephanie go to the cockpit, she started mentally reviewing emergency procedures. She knew they were on approach to the Atlanta airport when she had heard the cockpit emergency signal. When Stephanie went forward, Doris knew there was definitely something wrong. Her memory zeroed in on the Emergency Procedures section of her In-Flight Service Handbook. The printed page came into focus.

Anticipated Emergency Landing

When time is very limited, the three most important items to check are seatbelts, seat backs, and tray tables. With addi-

tional time, check smoking, explain bracing position (or yell
GRAB ANKLES), and assign exits and alternate exits.

Doris was mentally preparing herself. The kids! George
will take good care of them, but I had so hoped to see Kimberly wear my wedding dress. Don't be silly, Doris . . . keep
calm. It probably won't even fit Kimberly . . . George was
right. Perhaps flying is not for mothers. Oh, this is probably nothing more than a broken light. We'll be able to land
just fine. I've got to remain calm. I am responsible for these
people. Wish they'd let us know what's going on. We're back
up into a cruising pattern. I felt the plane climb about the
time Steph went forward. Hope the passengers didn't notice.
They seem undisturbed. Oh, think, Doris, think! What are
the emergency procedures? Ah! Here comes Stephanie!

As Stephanie moved from the cockpit down the aisle, she
motioned for the flight attendants to come aft to the buffet
area. Among the junior attendants was Charles, a lumbering,
happy-go-lucky guy who loved his career in the sky. Charles
had been one of the first men hired to become a flight attendant and he was performing excellently. As he made his
way back, he smiled so sincerely that any worries among the
passengers were extinguished.

Inside the buffet, Stephanie announced, "It's a possible
wheels up. The indicator light isn't signaling that the landing
gear is down. We're circling the control tower to let the fellows try to see if the gear's visible."

She was interrupted by the Intercom bell. The three soft
signals seemed frighteningly urgent. Grabbing the instrument, Stephanie heard, "Prepare for a belly landing. We'll
give you as much time as possible. We're going to circle a
couple more times and manually try to dislodge the gear, but
get ready."

Stephanie ticked off responsibilities in a firm voice.

"You all know the procedure. Keep calm. Give concise
instructions after we land. Evacuate passengers as quickly
as possible, not leaving the aircraft until the last passenger.
Take the first aid kit. Allow no smoking during or after land-

ing. Assemble passengers at a safe distance from aircraft and render all possible aid to passengers. Post guards to see that no mail, baggage or parts of the aircraft are disturbed. Notify the nearest company office as soon as possible. Make a complete detailed report, each of you. Make no comment to press or radio and refer all questions to our public relations and do all possible to cooperate with the FAA (Federal Aviation Administration) until Southaire releases us. Now go to your duties."

After stepping through the procedure, Stephanie quickly ordered her team into action.

"Charles, you and Doris start providing initial information to passengers. Janie, you check seat belts, straighten seat backs, fold tray tables and get all cigarettes extinguished. I'll choose, brief and reseat exit assistants. I know we have one blind man and two kids traveling unaccompanied. I'll get helpers for them. Charles, as soon as you and Doris finish explaining and showing bracing positions, be sure to have them remove sharp objects, pens, dentures, glasses and necklaces and tell them to remove their shoes. Remember, ladies should remove their stockings to prevent leg burns. Janie, as soon as you have finished, go back through and secure all loose objects in the cabin and buffet. Put everything in the lavatories. Work as fast as you can and then get to your jump seats and assume crash position. Good luck, kids."

Approaching the twelve year old traveling alone, Stephanie found a capable looking career woman in her thirties seated behind the girl. She asked her to take charge of the child. Seats were exchanged and the career woman was satisfactorily seated behind the emergency exit row door seats with the child beside her. The cabin was beginning to take on the appearance of a dress rehearsal for a suspense movie. A few of the passengers were visibly shaken and upset, but all were responding to the commands from the efficient Southaire attendants. The Captain had made a public announcement telling the passengers that the flight was experiencing difficulty with the landing gear.

Steward Charlie hoisted a two year old across a seat to be placed crosswise in another adults lap with a blanket wrapped about his head. The worried Mother was traveling with two toddlers and a passenger behind had been selected to assist her.

A signal alerted the cabin for another public announcement. The Captain's voice came over the system. "Ladies and Gentlemen, we will be experiencing a wheels-up landing at Hartsfield International airport in Atlanta. By now your capable attendants will have instructed you as to emergency landing procedures. Please do as you are told. We are approaching our landing pattern now. Will you please assume safety positions now and try to remain calm. Attendants, please buckle yourselves into your jump seats and assume emergency positions at once."

Stephanie caught a glimpse of the ground as the wounded plane approached. Glistening white foam blanketed the runway, and brightly colored emergency vehicles waited at the sidelines, their red and yellow lights flashing like a macabre carnival. Tiny figures stood by, fireman and ambulance attendants all watching the huge machine angle down. Tons of sheet metal meshed with unyielding concrete as the DC-8 jet slid in screaming complaint along runway 27 for half a mile. The cabin was filled with noise and motion.

Inside passengers were jolted. Heads bumped against forward seats. A handbag that had been over-looked careened through the cabin. The first aid kit skittered down the aisle. The screaming of a youngster added to the noise of the tearing belly of the giant ship. Then all was still. A blast of sirens pierced the eerie dawn while traces of sunshine filtered in to touch the stunned passengers inside.

Charles was the first attendant to move. He hopped up and in a booming voice shouted, "Okay folks, roller coaster ride is over. Let's use all the exits and move out quickly. We gotta make room for the next crowd to take this ride."

The other attendants stationed themselves at their designated exits, calmly urging passengers out. Within 90 seconds the plane was emptied. Charles could be heard directing the halting, shaken people. "Move quickly, no smoking, keep moving!"

When only a few passengers were left at her exit, Doris looked around to determine if she should redirect from another door, but the exodus was going smoothly. When the last passenger was evacuated, Stephanie got the first aid kit and the megaphone, then shouting for everyone to get off, she followed Doris out a wing exit. Charles booming instructions could be heard clearly without benefit of megaphone as he assembled passengers and started helping load them onto arriving ambulances and emergency vehicles.

As far as Stephanie could see, no one was seriously injured. There was one man cradling his right arm in his left hand with a possible break, and a few cuts were evident, but all the passengers and crew were on their feet despite their wobbly knees.

Within twenty minutes the area was cleared and attendants and crews were in the Southaire crew bus headed for general offices to meet CAA (Civil Aviation Administration) inspectors and company officials. During the interminable questions, Stephanie chided the Captain, "I can understand you wanting to break up the boredom of a long flight, but don't do it this way. There's too much paperwork!"

It was shortly after noon before the exhausted attendants could wearily make their way homeward.

When relating the story to her family, Doris told George about the blind man. "And you know what his remark was just before he left the crash scene?" She grinned. "He said, *Gee, that was fun. The last time I flew we didn't have this much fun.* "

The flight attendants were not given extra time off. Within two days Doris and Stephanie met in the stewardess lounge to prepare their clipboards for a rotation trip to Detroit. After the attendants were in the cabin, Danny Throckmorton, who had been scheduled by an agent in Atlanta for the Detroit destination, boarded the plane. The friendly brown-eyed youngster was seven years old. Traveling alone, his face wore bandages and multiple stitches. After the child was seated, the agent drew Stephanie aside.

"He's just gotten out of emergency at Grady Hospital. He and his father were in a horrible auto accident. His father was killed, but Danny doesn't know it yet. The Mother requested that we not inform her son. She wants to tell him when she gets him home. The father's casket is on this flight, in the baggage compartment. You're gonna have to be careful with this one. He adores his father and keeps asking a lot of questions about his Dad. He thinks Dad is still in the hospital and will be coming home later."

Stephanie squeezed her eyes shut. "Ouch! That's rough. Poor little fellow. We'll take good care of him. Is his Mother meeting us?"

"Yes and she wants to tell him herself, so be on guard and don't let anything slip about the father. He's a sweet kid and he's sharp."

Stephanie held a whispered conference with her co-workers and told them about Danny. He was traveling in first class which was Stephanie's bailiwick as senior stewardess. Doris was working senior in the coach section, and Doris assured Stephanie if she got a moment, she would talk with Danny also in hopes of making him have a super flight.

Once airborne, Stephanie took a few minutes to talk to Danny and to reassure him that she would be there in case he got frightened about traveling alone. She also cautioned him that they would be making stops in Chattanooga, Tennessee, Lexington, Kentucky, and Cincinnati, Ohio before they reached Detroit, and for him not to leave the airplane.

"But my mommy is going to meet me."

"Sure. Your mom will be in Detroit, but we have to stop other places first. So you just stay in this seat when we do."

"My daddy is in the hospital. We had an accident."

"Yes, I know you had an accident."

"My daddy will be home on another airplane."

Stephanie felt a lump form in her throat. She quickly eased out of the seat next to Danny. "I have work to do now. I'll bring you something to eat in a few minutes."

Inside the buffet Stephanie was surprised at the reaction she was having to the boy. Her emotions overcame her thoughts of duties as she sipped a glass of water and stared at cloud formations out the tiny buffet door window. *When Danny started talking about his father, I thought I was going to cry. I'm not sure I can be around him this entire flight. This is really getting to me and I thought I was tough. Well, got to serve this meal, got to get control.*

During her busy duties, Stephanie found moments to chat with Danny, but each time he made a remark about his Dad, she couldn't forget that Daddy's body was traveling beneath them. Danny's eyes were so wide and so brown that Stephanie felt like she was looking into pools of melting chocolate. When they were coming into Lexington, Stephanie sat beside Danny.

"When is your birthday, little friend?"

"I just had it. My trip with Dad was my birthday present, one of my presents. I also got a big train that goes around on a track and Daddy put it in the middle of the floor and we played with it. When my Daddy comes home, we are gonna build a table for it with trees and houses and everything."

Stephanie couldn't stand it. Even though they were coming in for landing, she jumped up and hurried to the stewardess jump seat.

As soon as they were on the ground, she hurried to the coach section to Doris. In whispered urgency, she told her friend. "We've got to change places. Danny is breaking my heart. I can't stand it. I'm ready to tell him the truth and let him have a good cry and get it over with. Doris, you're gonna have to take over front cabin and take care of him."

"Why, of course Stephanie. Bless his heart. I'll be glad to swap. How's he really doing?"

"Oh he's a fine little traveler and he doesn't make any demands. It's just me. Every time I sit down by him and try to visit, I get all choked up. I really can't understand it. I guess the situation is getting to me. I mean, really getting to me. Guess it's time for me to quit working with all these people and move on up to the cockpit where I only have to contend with the control panel."

"Ya know, Steph, if any woman can do it, you can."

Suddenly Stephanie's eyes filled to overflowing. She sniffed, muttered "damn it" and hurried to one of the lavatories.

Doris stood staring at her partner's back. She just discovered she has a heart, too. That's gotta be hard on her. Well, Steph's tough. She'll get over it. I better hike myself forward.

Doris talked with Danny as much as possible from Lexington throughout the flight, including the stop in Cincinnati, all the way to Detroit. Whenever he talked about his Daddy, Doris bit her cheek and let him talk. She felt that if he talked of the happy times with his father, then his memory would dwell on these same times when he learned of his father's death.

After the passengers had deplaned, an agent brought out Danny's mom. Boarding, she asked Doris, "Does he know?"

"No. No one told him. He doesn't know. And please accept our deepest sympathy. Danny's a wonderful little boy. He'll make it, and all of us from Southaire sincerely wish the best for you."

Before Mrs. Throckmorton could respond, she was in the embrace of her excited son.

"Hi Mom, boy, have Daddy and I got a lot to tell you. Did you know we had a car wreck?"

Both Doris and Stephanie gave Danny and his mom a farewell hug as they left the plane.

A few weeks later, returning from Los Angeles on a night coach, Doris noticed a strange smell in the cabin. She started sniffing, trying to locate the source but couldn't find it. She went forward and signaled Stephanie.

"Hey, come back here a minute when you get a chance. It's the strangest smelling cigarette or cigar or something. Somebody's got something really stinking up the area in coach. With 250 passengers, it's hard to pin point it. Stephanie walked back, sniffed and laughed. "It's marijuana."

By this time a woman passenger had lit another cigarette and the aqua smoke drifted casually from her nose. Stephanie nudged Doris and said, "There she is, big as life. Have fun."

Doris approached the thin, sun-tanned brunette and said, "Please don't smoke marijuana on this plane. It's against the law. Extinguish it, please."

"I'm not in the jurisdiction of any state. I'm not breaking anybody's law. I'm flying over the states." She took a puff of the cigarette and blew smoke in Doris's direction. "Does the airline have any specific rules against smoking pot?"

Flabbergasted, Doris moved backward and replied, "I don't know. I'll have to go look in my handbook, but I suggest you stop it. It is bothering the other passengers. Please put it out now."

The brunette threw Doris a menacing look, while she reached forward and tapped a balding man on top of his head. "Hey, is my smoking bothering you? Am I making too much noise with my smoking? Am I offensive?"

Meekly he turned, saw her flashing gray eyes and answered, "No, you're not bothering me."

Doris reported the incident to senior stewardess Saranata. Stephanie was mildly amused but Doris was insistent. "Steph, it is annoying. The whole cabin reeks. You carry more weight than I do. You go ask her to stop."

Stephanie approached the gray-eyed puffer and suggested she wait until she was off the plane before lighting any more cigarettes.

With an arrogant smirk, she offered the stewardess one. "Here, dearie, have a joint. It'll uncork your corkscrew."

"No thank you, and I strongly suggest you not smoke anymore."

The woman leaned forward and grabbed Stephanie's hand. "Has anyone ever told you that you have gorgeous eyes?"

Stephanie jerked her hand away. "Give me the rest of your cigarettes, please. I'll return them after we land."

Reluctantly she reached into her purse, but then quickly withdrew an empty hand. "Smoking pot relaxes me. If I can't smoke pot, I'll scream. I'll show you how I scream." She smirked and then screamed at the top of her lungs.

Her shriek brought comments from startled passengers around her. "What in the hell was that?" . . . "What's wrong?" . . . "Oh, what was that?"

Very calmly, the thin, nervous woman sighed and looked at Stephanie with dazed eyes. "If I can't smoke, I just get so tense. If you don't let me smoke, I'll just scream like that."

Stephanie said to no one in particular as she walked away. "I give up!" She went to the cockpit and described the incident to her Captain, while Doris and the other attendants tried to offer explanations to the other passengers as to what was going on.

The Captain expressed concern and told Stephanie he would call security people to meet the flight in Dallas. A younger, hipper copilot interrupted. "Is she sitting in the smoking section?" Stephanie nodded. "Then leave her alone. She's within her rights. She bought a ticket for the smoking section and she's smoking in the smoking section, so she's within her rights."

The stony-faced Captain commanded. "Just leave her alone. We're almost in and I'm going to have security meet her because she's breaking the law. You don't need to get involved anymore."

Stephanie had a worried expression on her face. Thoughtfully she replied, "I don't think we should turn people in. I don't think that's right. Even though she's annoying people, she doesn't deserve to have cops meeting her at the airport. Think of her civil rights."

The Captain, in his authoritative manner, told her, "I'm from the old school, Miss Saranata, and when I know of a law-breaker, I turn them in. Don't worry. It is now out of your hands. As Captain aboard this aircraft, I relieve you of further duties regarding this woman. You may return to your other passengers."

Chided, but not appeased, Stephanie had conflicting thoughts regarding the pot smoker. *Maybe I ought to warn the woman. I don't like the idea of cops meeting her. I believe she's harmless.*

But the harmless woman was making a pest of herself in the rear cabin. She giggled and sang and offered everyone a puff, threatening to scream every time Doris walked by and gave her a disapproving look.

Just before landing the woman announced in a loud voice, "I simply must go make myself more beautiful." She reached under her seat for a make-up case and started up the aisle toward the lavatories. Swinging the case, she said, "Hi there!" to about every third passenger along the way. She started to turn in the aisle to say something to someone when she lost her balance. Lurching down the aisle and falling, she banged her traveling case against a seat. It sprang the lock spilling the contents. Lipstick and comb were lost among a pile of small plastic bags filled with green-gray leaves.

Stephanie was near her when she fell, still wondering what to do about warning the woman. When she saw the bag spill its contents, immediately her thoughts changed. From a sympathetic observer, she became an indignant citizen and thought, *It's okay for her to smoke the darn stuff, but if she's a pusher, then I'll help the cops put her away.*

Under the guise of assisting the woman, Stephanie kicked one of the packets of marijuana under a seat. After the woman was steadied and sent on her way with assistance from a junior attendant, Stephanie reached under the seat and placed the packet in her pocket.

When security people met the plane, Stephanie told the authorities what she had seen. She produced the packet and the officers asked her to accompany them to police headquarters to make a statement for booking the woman.

As she bid Doris so long, Stephanie griped, "Boy, I do my duty and I get to go trekking along to the police station. Here it is four o'clock in the morning. I've been up since eight o'clock yesterday. This is what I get for being helpful!"

Doris laughed. "Yeah, but just think, Steph, you're involved and that's your cup of tea."

"Well, it's sure better than getting up in four hours to make breakfast for George, the monsters, and checking to make sure they all brush-em, brush-em."

"Bye Steph."

"Bye Doris."

Chapter 22—Atlanta to Miami
by way of Hawaii

When Stephanie finally reached her apartment about nine in the morning, she was too exhausted to sleep. She was desperately hungry and pulled a large sirloin steak from the freezer that she was saving in the event she wanted to invite someone. Just as she slid the steak into the oven broiler, her phone rang. She hesitated. She was in the mood for a good, hot, solitary meal with no interruptions. But curiosity overcame her and she lifted the receiver.

His booming voice almost made the instrument unnecessary. "Hey, Sis, what'cha doing?"

"Hi Pop. I'm sound asleep and you woke me."

"That's alright. Get up. I got something for you to do."

"I got something to do, too. Sleep!"

"C'mon, c'mon. You're awake. I bought a plane in Atlanta."

"You in Atlanta, Pop?"

"No! No! That's why I'm calling you. I can't get any of these air jocks that work fer me to get their hightails up to Hotlanta to fetch my new plane. I want you should bring it down fer me. And it's time you paid your Mother and me a little visit anyway. I'll pay your pass fee back to Atlanta when you pilot my new Comanche down here."

"Gee Pop, you'll pay my whole service charge for my pass . . . the whole $8.27? Wow!"

"Can it, Sis, you know what I mean. I want you to bring my aero-plane."

"Tell me, honestly Mac, do you want to see me or do you just want a ferry pilot?"

"Damn skirt. You're just like your Mother. Pauline was right. We should have drowned you at birth. Of course I wants to see my baby girl. Now give me a run down on your schedule so's I'll know when youse is coming."

"Hold on a minute, Mac."

"What's the matter, don't you know your schedule?"

"It isn't that. I gotta go turn my steak."

'Steak? What steak? I thought youse said youse was asleep."

Stephanie gave no answer. She turned her steak and went back to the telephone. Knowing she had a five day off period after her next flight, Stephanie held the instrument a moment thinking. Then she spoke. "Pop, I can bring your plane, but not right away. I'll go out tomorrow to the airport and check on your purchase, but then I have one more trip to work, just a quickie turn-around. Then I can ferry it down to Florida for you. You'll have to call the hanger folks and give me authorization for your plane before I can fly it down for you. And Mac, I want my trip logged. You know I only need 20 more hours before I can qualify for my commercial license and this will be a good way for me to log a few more solo hours."

"Sure, sure, no problem. I can handle that okay. When ya comin?"

"Let's see, this is Thursday morning. I can come down Sunday. That's when I start my five days off. But listen Mac, I want to fly it around here a tad bit to get used to it before I head toward Sarasota, so it might be late Sunday afternoon when I get in. I'll radio ahead and let you know my ETA. Hold on a minute and let me rescue my cow burning in the broiler."

"How come you eating so much this time of the day? Ya pregnant?"

"Don't you wish? You'd make a darling Gram Pa Pa."

"Bunk! Don't you come at me with none of those foolish notions."

She turned off the broiler and left her steak, crossing her fingers that it wouldn't get tough while awaiting her knife and fork. "Okay boss man, give me my orders."

Her heart was thumping with excitement and sleep was a lost thought. She tackled the hunk of meat and made mental plans to get in as much flying time as possible during the time off when she would be taking the new Comanche down to Florida. She planned to fly it around the Georgia area to log as many solo hours as possible before she flew it to Florida.

On late Sunday afternoon, when she finally taxied up to her father's charter air service hanger, she had accumulated several fuel bills but had gotten in more than her required number of solo hours to qualify for her commercial license. As she alighted from the cockpit, Mac grabbed her in a war whoop.

After they were seated in his office, she presented him with the wad of expense receipts, reminding him that he'd said he would cover whatever it cost her to fly the plane down to Florida.

He looked at them with disbelief and exclaimed, "How in the hell did you come? By way of Hawaii? You damn skirt! You're all alike. You can think of the damndest ways to spend my money!" The twinkle in his crinkling eyes made his anger a sham, and Stephanie knew the rapport between them still meant the same thing . . . *we're just alike.*

Greeting Pauline in their spacious Florida retirement home, Stephanie was again impressed by her mother and her surroundings. Pauline was still exquisite. She had changed little from her early photographs in the first Southaire stewardess uniform some thirty-four years past. Her frosted wind blown auburn hair framed the gently lined, tanned complexion, and her aquamarine eyes were livelier than ever. Her figure retained its youthful lines and she could boast of being one of the Sarasota Country Club single's tennis champions.

Their home was extensively decorated with souvenirs collected from all over the world. Upon his retirement from Southaire, Mac was presented a life-time airline pass for himself and his wife. Pauline carefully planned their worldwide vacation trips each year and some of the mementoes of their travels were quite valuable. Their home had been opened for several local charity tours and the only room not permitted on view was Mac's den. Pauline kept the door

closed and bid their maid to enter once a week with a large
garbage can to carry out the remains of Mac's wallowing in
his so-called study.

The greeting by mother and daughter swelled Mac's heart
with pleasure and he looked from one to the other. Stephanie
held her mom at arm's length and whistled at Pauline.

"You look fantastic. When are you going to come back
to work? My partner is a married woman . . . and you know
you're always saying that you'd do anything to get away from
Dad . . . and you're the best looking stewardess that Southaire ever had."

"Oh darling, you're so sweet. I have entertained the notion of returning to that career, but I have so many projects
that need me. I have the League of Women's voters, underprivileged children, Gray Panther group, this tennis cham-
pionship reputation, and numerous luncheons to attend. Returning to Southaire as a stewardess just isn't feasible at this
time. However, if your father doesn't conform to my sage
advice on not cornering the charter service of Florida, then
perhaps I will submit an application and hope to be based in
Chicago or some other distant metropolitan area."

"Ha! Pop'd never let you go."

With a wink at Mac, Pauline continued, "However,
Stephanie, you have added fuel to my fantasies. I could do
it, you know. As a matter of assumption, if I went back
with full seniority, I would definitely fly A-line and be your
constant supervisor. There's a real adjustment I would arbi-
trarily suggest to Southaire immediately upon their acceptance of my application. I would most assuredly request a
hot-pants uniform. Southaire is so static and antiquated in
their designers. Their uniforms are too conservative. What
they need is a delightful short pants outfit with perhaps a
halter top."

"MOTHER!"

Mac shouted, "Yeah, I'd gofer dat!" Then forgetting Pauline's wink, he looked questioningly at Pauline. "Youse ain't
serious? You old bags need to stay at home. A woman's place

is at home. If women gotta be on the airplane, they should be gorgeous . . . in gorgeous uniforms."

"But Pop, Mom is gorgeous and she would be an asset to Southaire. As a matter of fact, she can have my job. I'm going to be a pilot for Southaire.

Pauline quickly looked at Stephanie. "Oh darling, I think that's perfectly marvelous. You are so capable to pilot Southaire's flights."

"I'm serious Mom. I'm gonna give it a try. I'm gonna give Southaire a run for it's money and if they won't hire me as a pilot, then I'm gonna find out why. With the time I just completed flying Pop's new airplane, I'm ready to go for my commercial. If I make it, move over boys, a female stewardess will be a female pilot for Southaire.

Mac stood stupefied. "I knew women was gonna take over dat cockpit some day. I just knew it. But damn! My own daughter! Listen Sis, if you really wanna fly, quit Southaire and come fly fer my outfit. I'll pay ya the same as I pay the jocks. I know you're good. I'll give you an even break on pool charters, meaning I'll let you put your hand in the job jar same as my boys and everything with be even-steven. What say? Ya wanna think about it? Ya don't wanna fly commercial airplanes for Southaire. Why, that's a man's job . . . should be anyway. You come on back down here to Florida and work fer me. After all, someday it will be your charter service anyway."

Pauline smiled knowingly and said, "McLain, Stephanie will do what is right for her. Darling, is there anything you desire during your welcomed visit at home?"

"Lots of rest, Mom . . . just lots of rest."

On Monday evening, just before she was ready to board an Atlanta homeward flight, Mac said goodbye to Stephanie. Pauline had been unable to cancel a meeting, so father and daughter were sharing the final minutes of her visit.

"Yer mother enjoyed seeing ya and I'm glad my plane's down here even if it has got so many more miles on it than I expected and you half wore it out getting it down here."

Cocking his head sideways he squinted his penetrating eyes and said, "Ya got your heart set on flying fer an airline or would ya think of taking over your old Pop's business?" Then with gruffness in his tone, he continued. "I ain't got a boy to take it over fer me and you're all I got, which ain't much cause you're a skirt, but at least you can fly a plane. Ya ain't wrecked one yet. I love ya, but I don't understand ya. If ya was a guy, you'd already be trying to take over my business."

Turning her full mouth down in a sympathetic understanding gesture, Stephanie replied. "I want bigger stuff than that, Mac. But I'll think about it."

His booming voice carried. "What's bigger than having your own airline business?"

Hugging his neck, she whispered, "Let me know, Pop, when you get a jet. I'm a jet-ager." As she started boarding she turned with a parting remark. "Maybe I'll just join a flying circus and be a wing walker."

When Stephanie and Doris met in the stewardess attendant lounge before boarding procedures, they talked about how they had spent their time off. After Stephanie gave a capsule description of her visit home, she taunted Doris. "And what did you do? Wash and iron the whole five days?"

"Oh, no. I took my jet recurrent review. You know, Stephanie, when I first returned to flying, I was really worried about the younger girls accepting me and if I would be able to re-learn all an attendant has to know. School was hard—very hard—and I had to study an awful lot. The six weeks I had to stay at the training center, away from my family, was rough on all of us. But now, like going back through recurrent jet review, it's all worthwhile. My family cooperates beautifully and George is marvelous at helping me study. When I'm in class all day with the younger girls and boys, they don't seem to resent me. As a matter of fact, they seem to go out of their way to be nice to me. Perhaps they feel sorry for me, but I honestly don't think so. I make as good or better grades than they do, and I really do know all that I'm supposed to know.

Anyhow, that's how I spent Friday and Saturday. Sunday I went to Six Flags amusement part with my family. Monday I washed and ironed."

During pre-boarding duties, an agent approached Stephanie with a black woman in a wheelchair, who appeared to be in her forties, followed by a young black man in overalls.

"This lady is going to Detroit and we wanted to board her early. This is her son. He will help you get her settled and then deplane before takeoff."

The man removed his workman's cap and said, "Howdy, ma'am. My Momma is going to Detroit to see a special doctor. I got a sister who lives in Detroit and she is gonna take care of Momma."

Together they moved the heavy, frightened woman from the wheelchair into a seat. Then Stephanie folded the chair and placed it in the closet. The young man stood near-by, holding cap in hands. "Momma has never flown before. I's never flown either. Sister sent the money for Momma to fly."

Stephanie tried to reassure him. "We get first-riders aboard all the time. It will be a pleasant experience for your Mother and don't you worry. We will take good care of her."

He reached into his overall pocket and pulled forth two crumpled dollar bills and handed them to Stephanie. "Please ma'am, could you see that Momma gets a drink of water?"

Stephanie handed him back the money. "Of course I'll see that she gets water and lunch and anything else that she wants. Don't you worry about her. She will be fine."

He hung his head. "Well Momma had a big breakfast."

Stephanie reached out and patted his sloping shoulder. "Please don't worry about your Mother. She will enjoy this trip and will write you all about it when she gets to Detroit. Now you quit worrying."

"Momma can't write."

"Well, I'll tell you what. You go home and stay by your telephone. When we get to Detroit, I'll pay for a call and your Momma can talk to you herself and tell you that she is alright."

"We don't got a phone, but a neighbor lady's got one. Wait. I'll write down the number. You'll really let Momma call me when she gets there?"

"I certainly will. You stay by this telephone and we will be calling you in just a few hours. I promise you, your Mother will call. Now please don't worry."

Ducking his head, he muttered, "Yes ma'am. Thank you."

After kissing his mother goodbye, he ambled off the plane. Turning to a junior attendant nearby, Stephanie spoke with anger in her voice without even realizing the color of his skin was the same as the meek passenger.

"You'd think that the last traces of this attitude would be gone, this poor man feeling that we weren't going to take care of his mother . . . that we wouldn't even give her a drink of water. Are things never going to change? How much longer will it take to change attitudes, how much longer must people fear humiliation?"

The junior stewardess grinned. "But ma'am, the laws have changed."

"It doesn't matter if the laws change . . . if the people won't change their minds and their attitudes. Oh, this just infuriates me. To think that poor young man, these poor people still live in a community where they don't know they are equals. He still has the idea that he isn't up to the white people standards. He felt like his mother wouldn't be treated like everyone else. That's what's wrong with this country!"

The black attendant she was lecturing to told Stephanie, "You tell 'em Tiger, but do it later, because right now we got a bunch of people coming at us clutching boarding passes and wanting something to eat."

That flight went smoothly, landing in Detroit right on time. True to her word, Stephanie placed a call to the number the young man had given her so his mother could call him and tell him all about the flight. The sister was present and said hi to her brother and assured him she would take good care of their mother.

The next time Stephanie entered the stewardess lounge, the attendants were all a flutter with exclamations. "Burt Reynolds is in town." . . . "He's doing a movie down in South Georgia and will be commuting through Atlanta while filming." . . . "Can you imagine, Burt Reynolds? . . . I'd just like to touch that man." . . . Another gal exclaimed quickly, "I'd like to have that man touch me."

Stephanie stood straddle-legged in front of them with her hands on her slim hips. "You're a bunch of nuts. I can't imagine a bunch of grown, responsible females getting so worked up about a movie star. Burt Reynolds isn't anything but a man doing a job and getting well paid for doing that job."

"Yeah, but what a man and what a job he is doing!" . . . "Hope I get him on my flight." . . . "If he shows up on my flight, I'll lock us both in the john and won't even let him come out for air." . . . "Man, if I was locked up with Burt Reynolds, I wouldn't have any air, I'd just hold my breath!

Stephanie gave them a disgusted look. "You're all cracked, flipped out gooses!" She stalked over to read the bulletin board.

One of the pilots came in. "Hey you broads, your fearless leader is in the terminal. The one and only Gloria Steinem is giving an interview near Southaire's ticket counter. Now don't all of you stampede me at once."

Some the seated attendants looked at him with casual interest. A few of them said, "So?"

Stephanie whirled from the bulletin board and shouted, "She's here, now?"

"Yeah, going out on our 1017 to New York."

Stephanie grinned and exclaimed, "Ya kidding? That's my flight. Oh boy, I can't believe this. I've got A-line. Terrific! Boy, I'm going to bend Ms. Steinem's ear. I've got a lot to tell her and a lot to ask her. Hey, I can't believe this. Are you sure she's on 1017?"

"Lady, I got no reason to lie."

There were snickers from the seated group. Someone said, "Hey Steph, what was it you said about celebrities? Give me Burt Reynolds any day. There's no accounting for some people's taste."

Stephanie whirled on them. "Listen you sap heads, I don't know how many of you are on my crew today but I'm giving you fair warning . . . you're gonna do all the work. I'm going to sit and talk to Gloria. One advantage of me being A-line is that I get to give the orders and I'm giving them in advance 'cause I want no interruptions. Now hear this . . ."

Everyone laughed as they started on their pre-flight duties gathering forms. That was one of Stephanie's favorite flights that day.

On their next rotation trip, Doris waited until they were checked into the hotel the first night before confiding to Stephanie. "George got laid off last week, but since I missed the last trip and I haven't had a chance to tell you. I had sorta been thinking about quitting, but now we're both glad I have this job."

"Oh Doris, I'm sorry to hear this."

"Well, you know how it is with an automotive job. In these times it's a bit unsteady."

"How does George feel?"

"Well gosh . . . he's relieved that I have a job. He doesn't have to go into immediate panic to find a temporary job to tide us over. Even though George is in a managerial position, he would be willing to do construction work or night watch-man or anything to take care of us, but now that I have this job, he doesn't have to do that. We've been putting most of my salary in savings, so now we have that to live on. And I make a pretty darn good salary, so we won't be too hurt by the lay-off."

"I didn't know you were thinking about quitting, Doris." Stephanie was sprawled across one of the twin beds.

Doris was sitting on the other bed with her hand on the telephone. "Yes, I was kinda thinking about it. I have been worried about keeping up with you younger girls and I have worried about my own two teenagers being without constant parental supervision. And George has sometimes not quite understood that I'm just as tired as he is. It's been an adjustment and sometimes there's conflict. The kids have been great, the way they have assumed responsibility and George has been helpful in most ways, but of course ever since we've been married, I've always been right there to take care of everything for him. He still finds it hard to realize that I'm not there constantly at his beck and call." A pensive Doris was letting Stephanie see a different side of her.

Stephanie pointed toward the telephone and said, "Speaking of a call, I suppose you still need to call George and report in like you do every trip. He knows you're alright and you're a big girl now. You don't have to report in."

"Oh, no, I must call home. I always call home. I always call them. They would all worry if I didn't. I'm not head of the household. George is, even though he isn't working right now. In fact, Steph," a smile played around her lips, "George is rather enjoying not working for a little while."

Stephanie chided good naturedly, "See I told you. What you're doing is important. You're your own woman and you're just as much head of the household as George. Make George be a good househusband. Make sure he gets your underwear put in your drawer while you're out slaving for money to feed the brood."

"Stephanie! You're hopeless! This isn't a major change for my family. It's good to learn how to adjust to inconsistencies of life. As a matter of fact, neither George nor I are worried. We're going to take a little vacation while he has some time off. I've swapped some trips to get a week off. We're going to San Francisco on a mileage pass, just the two of us, just for some fun. We're enjoying the situation but it really hasn't changed our status. George will always be head of the household and he will be recalled as the major wage earner for our family as soon as the union gets through negotiating."

"Well I just hope to hell he is there to meet you with a shaker of martinis when you get home from work. And if I were you, I'd certainly insist that he have on a clean apron!"

"Stephanie, get off my sore back. Go find yourself a man!"

When Stephanie and Doris stepped out of the elevator in the hotel lobby in search of dinner, a shrill voice assaulted them. "Doris? Doris Spencer? Doris! I can't believe that's you . . . but I'd know you anyplace."

They turned to greet a short chubby blonde woman approaching them with arms outstretched. Doris stepped forward and was engulfed in a grunting bear hug and muffled sounds of, "Glory! What a surprise!"

Doris turned and indicated, "Uh, this is Stephanie Saranata and you're, uh, wait, I think I know."

"Sure you do, honey. We graduated from stewardess class together and flew a lot of trips together."

"Uh, which stewardess class?"

"What do you mean which stewardess class? The best one Southaire ever graduated . . . the class of fifty-four."

"Now I know! You're Penny Perkins. Golly, Penny, it's been ages since I've seen you."

"Yeah, quite a few. Doris you look suburb, so tiny and elegant, or rather, elegant is the word. You look just like you did twenty years ago. I don't know what you're doing, but it's working."

Stephanie shook hands with Penny. "You two flew together in the fifties?"

Penny bubbled, "Sure did, it was a great job and loved every minute of it. Didn't we Doris?"

"We really did, Penny, and guess we still do love it."

"Yeah, I know what you mean. I treasure my memories too. I still do love flying. But I never get to do much of it anymore. Say, can I buy you gals a drink? I'm just killing time until Jody gets back."

Doris inquired, "Jody?"

"Ah yes, my precious Jody. Jody Stinsen. I'm Mrs. Jody Stinsen and have been that for about eighteen or so years now. Lordy, how the time flies. But Doris I can't get over how great you look. Say, am I interrupting anything?"

"No, we were just going out to dinner. Would you like to join us, Penny?"

Doris glanced at Stephanie. Stephanie supported her invitation saying, "We'd be delighted to have you along, Penny."

"Gee thanks Stephanie, but Jody is coming back to get me in a little while to take me out for a play . . . Noel Coward in Two Keys. Jody and I are just up here for vacation. He's done pretty well ranching all these years and has started dabbling in the stock market. So one fine day he says, well, since I am playing the stock market, let's just go to market. So here we are in New York City playing the role of tourist. First time I've been back since Jane and I came through here on our way back from Europe. Jody and I were married shortly after that trip, and all these years we've been too busy to get back this way. Seems a lot different to be here as a tourist than as a crew member. What are you doing here?"

Doris and Stephanie exchanged glances. Stephanie said, "Excuse me a moment. I need to make a call."

As she walked away, Doris smiled. "Penny, believe it or not, I'm here as a crew member again."

"You kidding, Doris Spencer? You been flying all this time? Why you must practically own Southaire."

"Oh no, no. I quit shortly after you did. I've only returned to flying about three years ago when they started rehires. You ought to give it a whirl, Penny. It's great, just about as much fun as it was when we flew before, only I think it's harder this time, a lot more work involved with the jets."

"Oh glory, Jody would crack his gourd if I even mentioned something like this. We've got five kids running around on the ranch and I have to ride herd on them."

"Five kids? I never pictured you with five children, Penny. You were such a bundle of energy and such a talker that I never thought you'd be quiet long enough to get pregnant."

"You don't have to be quiet to get pregnant, Doris."

Doris laughed and looked around for Stephanie and saw that she was engrossed in conversation with a bell hop.

"Penny, guess I better get Stephanie and go eat. We've got a four AM call and it's already after eight. Tomorrow is a day of flying that you wouldn't believe. We'll travel more miles tomorrow than you and I used to travel all week. It was really great seeing you again. Oh, by the way, you mentioned Jane. Do you two still keep in touch? I once had a passenger ask about her for some reason or other. Seems he was editor of one of the farm magazines and he told me about his run in with her. Guess she made quite an impression on him. Anyway, he's still traveling with Southaire."

"Believe it or not, Jane's in Lexington, Kentucky . . . a professor, mind you. She married a real smart fellow, then went back to school herself. Went on to get a Master's degree, then got a Doctor's degree and now she's a department head at Lexington University. We still write occasionally and exchange pictures at Christmas. She and her husband don't get along too well, but they haven't gotten a divorce. Can't understand that. There are no children involved but then, it's none of my business."

"Well, next time you write, mention me to her. It was really nice seeing you again, Penny. Come fly with us."

"I will, but only as a passenger."

Conclusion

Doris had been pressuring Stephanie to take jet recurrent training.

"Well, I was hoping to hear something so I wouldn't have to take it. It's really a waste of Southaire's money for me to go through that session," Stephanie said.

"Steph, sometime I just don't understand you. Every flight attendant has to go through jet recurrent and you know that you're way past due for it."

"I already know all of my safety procedures for all types of jet aircraft, Doris good buddy. I can pass recurrent with both hands tied behind me. And I'm really not interested in giving up a couple of days to sit in that kind of a classroom and review jet procedures. I have other plans for my time."

"Steph, what's going on? Why do you think you should be exempt from the review session and testing?"

"Don't want to talk about it. I'll let you know as soon as I can. Doris, it's something important. It does have to do with me not taking jet recurrent, but I honestly can't discuss it right now."

As they entered the crew lounge, their frowning Chief Stewardess, Joan Martin, beckoned for Stephanie.

"Stephanie, come in my office, please."

Doris poked her friend. "See, I told you to sign up for recurrent."

Stephanie grimaced, shrugged her shoulders and went into her supervisor's office. The supervisor, Joan, started talking as Stephanie approached her desk.

"Couldn't I wait a little longer? I'm hoping something will come up to make this training unnecessary."

Joan, in exasperation, said, "Stephanie, I don't know what you're talking about, although personnel has asked me for your files, but if you plan to keep flying for Southaire you have to take jet recurrent training."

Smiling Stephanie reassured her immediate boss. "Well I definitely plan to keep flying for Southaire, so where do I sign up?"

Joan was looking at Stephanie quizzically but maintaining her authoritative demeanor. "Be at the flight training center 0800 Monday. As you will probably remember from having taken the course every year since you've been with Southaire, it is a testing review of the L-1011, 727, Super 727, 747, Super 9, Super 8, the 10 and all the stretch models we now have in service. Here are the required manuals so you can memorize them over the weekend."

Stephanie took the yellow bound pamphlets and stood up to leave. Joan also stood.

"Stephanie, I don't know what you've got brewing, but whatever it is, I want to wish you good luck."

"Thank you, Joan, I'll need it."

Stephanie was all fluid motion as she reentered the lounge area. All she had really heard in the office had been that personnel had sent for her files. Doris grinned when she saw the books in her friend's hand. "Finally got caught, huh? There's no way you can get out of it now."

"Wouldn't bet on that. This is only Thursday and class isn't until Monday. But even if I do have to take the refresher course, it will be a snap." She opened the book at random. "Look at this. How do you apply the Heimlich Maneuver?"

Doris inquired, "Well do you know how to apply it when a person is choking? Statistics show that almost 4,000 people died last year just from choking."

"Certainly, I know but I doubt if I'll ever use the knowledge. You stand behind the victim and wrap your arms around his waist. Allow his head, arms and upper torso to hang forward. Grasp your fist with your other hand and place the fist against the victim's abdomen, slightly above the navel and below the rib cage. Press your fist forcefully into the victim's abdomen with a quick upward thrust. Repeat several times, if necessary."

Stephanie rattled on, "When the victim is sitting, the rescuer stands behind the victim's chair and performs the maneuver in the same manner."

"Stephanie! That's terrific. I missed that question on my recurrent. I found out I didn't know as much as I thought I did once I got into the testing."

"I know all the first aid procedures by heart. Sending me through this is wasting company money. Any good stewardess already knows 95 percent of this stuff." She thumped the pamphlets in her hand.

"Well," Doris said, "I think recurrent training is necessary. We do tend to forget if we don't use methods frequently."

"They really should be educating us more about the mechanics of the planes we are on. I'm sure glad I know how to operate a plane. Every flight attendant should have at least some elementary pilot training."

Doris chuckled. "You could have a point there, Steph. It makes sense but those guys in the cockpit probably wouldn't be too thrilled about it."

"Those guys, as you say, in the cockpit are going to have to learn to accept change or get out."

"Steph, what are you talking . . .?

Halfway to the exit door, she motioned to Doris, "Come on, we've got to get this flight ready."

Doris was transferring clothes from the washer to dryer on Monday when the ringing telephone interrupted.

"Why Steph, this is a coincidence. I was going to call you tonight to tell you our good news. George has gone back to work."

"Terrific! Seems like this is everyone's lucky day."

"Hey, it just dawned on me. Aren't you supposed to be in recurrent this morning? Is something wrong?"

"Nooooo, everything's great! I told you I'd get out of recurrent, didn't I?"

"Stephanie, you sound funny. Have you been drinking? Did you get fired?"

"Don't you know Southaire can't fly without me?"

"Well, I know it but I didn't think management did."

"I'm serious Doris! They literally can't fly without me."

"Steph, I think I'm missing something in this conversation. You're not in jet recurrent. You haven't been fired. Just where are you?"

"Right at this moment I'm at the phone in crew lounge and I'm trembling. Had to call you! Doris . . . I've been accepted for pilot training!"

"You've what? Well, I'll be damned!"

"I'm now officially a Southaire pilot trainee. Course I'll have to fly Engineer first . . . but eventually I'll move up in seniority and be copilot and then, Doris, as soon as I can, I'm gonna be the first female Southaire Captain."

"Oh, Steph! I'm so happy for you." The initial shock wearing off, Doris was eager for details. "But how did you do it? When did you do it? Why didn't you tell me before?"

"It wasn't easy. I had to really sell them on my qualifications. Some string pulling by my Dad might have made it easier, but . . . pardon the pun . . . I didn't want to fly in on his coattails."

She paused and the excitement made her voice break. "I've had my application in for a month. They are short pilots and I knew this. That's why I've been so jumpy lately. I couldn't tell anyone until I was sure I had the job. This is something I want to do all by myself. You understand, don't you?"

"Yes, I do. Gee, I'm going to miss you Steph, but I always knew you had big things ahead of you. Oh, Steph, I think I'm going to cry."

"Don't you dare, Doris. If you cry, I might and I'm in the middle of a bunch of pilots. It's going to be hard enough for these guys to accept me. But a blubbering female pilot is more than they can cope with right now. I have to help them raise their consciousness, first."

"If anyone can do it, you can. Go get 'em, Stephanie Saranata. Be Southaire's first female pilot!